DIRECTIONS IN DEVELOPMENT

Integration of Transport and Trade Facilitation

Selected Regional Case Studies

T. R. Lakshmanan
Uma Subramanian
William P. Anderson
Frannie A. Léautier

THE WORLD BANK
WASHINGTON, D.C.

Contents

Foreword

Globalization trends worldwide are shrinking distances, enabling countries to connect through markets, trade, information, finance and investment. Technological advances in information, communication and transportation have facilitated these processes. Alongside, numerous regional trade blocs have emerged, as countries seek comparative advantages and ease their entry in to world markets.

Developing countries face a unique opportunity to participate competitively in this global and regional production and trading system, offering value-added services, skills resident in their human resources, as well as other resources. However, this opportunity depends on the ability of these countries to meet international market standards that increasingly emphasize high quality and just-in-time delivery.

This book examines experiences of interrelated transport and trade integration in selected regional trade blocs. The case studies range from advanced systems (Europe and North America) to more nascent efforts (Southern Africa and South Asia). The genesis for this book comes from an international workshop on transport and trade facilitation sponsored by the World Bank/ESCAP (Economic and Social Commission for Asia and the Pacific). The workshop was a forum for policy dialogue with government and private sector stakeholders in South Asia as these countries are beginning to position themselves to participate in regional and global markets.

Creating and maintaining efficient regional transport and trade facilitation systems are complex tasks that are often politically sensitive, since they involve both infrastructure provision and management as well as infrastructure policy issues. However, such systems are crucial if the transport and logistics gaps are not to adversely influence critical economic sectors, that in turn would affect economic growth, employment and therefore, poverty.

We hope that this book would provide guidance and increase the knowledge base for developing countries and regions during these periods of transition.

James P. Bond
Acting Vice President
Private Sector Development and Infrastructure
The World Bank

Acknowledgments

This report was prepared under the task team leadership of Uma Subramanian. The authors for various chapters are T.R. Lakshmanan, William P. Anderson, Frannie A. Léautier, and Uma Subramanian. We gratefully acknowledge inputs from Marc Juhel, Ron Kopicki, and Stephan von Klaudy. Gladys Stevens provided administrative assistance.

1

Transport and Trade Facilitation: An Overview

T. R. Lakshmanan

Technology has been a major driver of globalization in recent times. Information technologies (IT)—representing a confluence of computer and communication technologies—are transforming transport and trade in the twenty-first century. Although trade and the spread of economic activities across national borders have been increasing for a century or more, new developments in the enabling and space-shrinking technologies of transportation and communication are fundamentally transforming space-time relationships worldwide.

These technologies make possible the management and coordination of globally distributed economic activities that are diverse in nature. They permit increasing division of labor in the production processes as the component activities are further disaggregated and spatially reallocated. This partition of production processes (the slicing of the "production value chain") across national borders results in different stages of production being carried out in many countries. Raw materials and components may come from two different countries, with assembly in a third, and marketing from yet other countries in response to consumer signals from around the world. Parts and components are "sourced" internationally (a process likely to be expanded with growing Internet use); they accounted for $800 billion in trade in the early 1990s (World Bank, 2000b). Indeed, the whole process is globally coordinated. A significant portion of global value added is in the resultant global production networks.

These networks offer economic opportunities to all countries, especially in the developing world. If they invest in transport and communication systems that are effective, developing countries can plug into these networks. They can benefit from the spatial dispersion of manufacturing activities and, over time, from the associated service activities—all of which lead to expanded trade. Trade growth confers on the develop-

1

ing countries the benefits of globalization—increased market access for their exports, acquisition of new technology through international transfers, and the efficiency gains in the overall economy resulting from increased competitive pressures.

Under the impetus of declining transport costs and declining tariffs, trade has grown much faster than income since World War II. During the 1990s, trade in goods and services grew twice as fast as global GDP. In an affluent economy such as that of the United States, trade grew three times as fast as GDP in the past quarter century. During the 1990s the share of global trade attributable to the developing countries climbed from 23 percent to 29 percent (World Bank, 2000b).

Indeed, international trade flows are penetrating deeper into the workings of most economies, linking them to one another and modifying their economic structure and productivity. In the increasingly competitive economic environment worldwide, more and more countries offer high-value and low-cost production capacity and speedy time-definite delivery of goods at competitive prices.

Regional Trading Blocs

In this context a surge has occurred in the formation of regional trading blocs. Each trade bloc represents a cluster of neighboring countries that link their economies and seek to create dynamic comparative advantages to facilitate their insertion in the global economy on favorable terms. Figure 1-1 compares the population and GNP of five regional trading blocs: the North American Free Trade Agreement (NAFTA) signatories (Canada, Mexico, and the United States), the fifteen-member European Union (EU), the Common Market of the South (*Mercado Comin del Sur* or Mercosur), the South Asian Association for Regional Cooperation (SAARC), and the Southern African Development Community (SADC).

The NAFTA signatories and the European Union represent the two largest economies at a global level. Mercosur—comprising Argentina, Brazil, Paraguay, Uruguay, and two associate members (Bolivia and Chile)—is the largest economy among developing economies. In population size, SAARC is dominant, with the NAFTA countries, the European Union, and Mercosur serving as medium-size regions.

Figure 1-2 shows intraregional trade as a share of total trade in the large trading blocs. It is a crude measure of the tendency to direct trade toward other bloc members.

Overview

The following chapters analyze the scope and status of the interrelated processes of trade and transport integration in all five trading blocs. For

Figure 1-1. Population and GNP of Case Study Economies, 1998

Population in millions

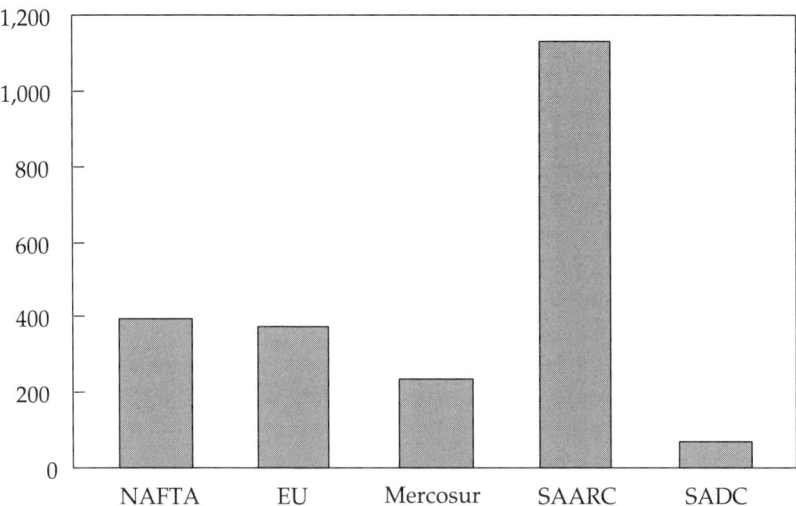

GNP in billions of U.S. dollars

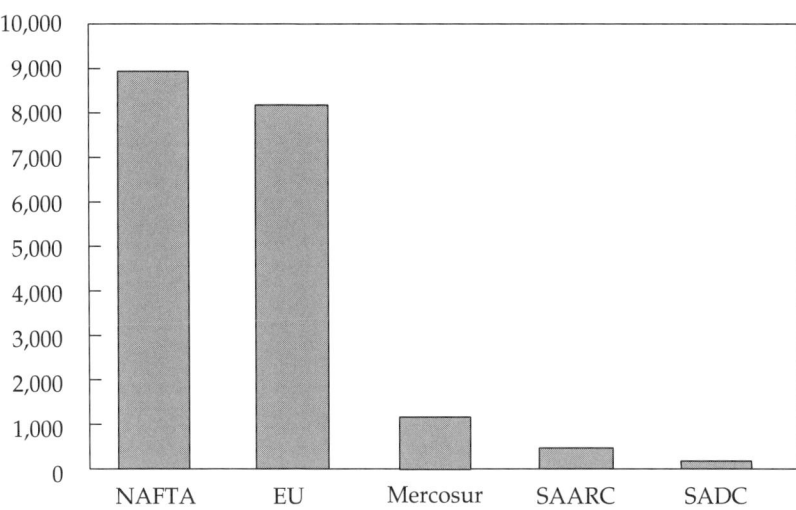

Note: The figure compares the economies of the North American Free Trade Agreement countries, the European Union, the Common Market of the South (Mercado Comin del Sur or Mercosur), the South Asian Association for Regional Cooperation, and the Southern African Development Community.
Source: World Bank (2000c).

Figure 1-2. Intraregional Trade as a Percentage of Total Trade in the Large Trading Blocs, 1962–94

Percent

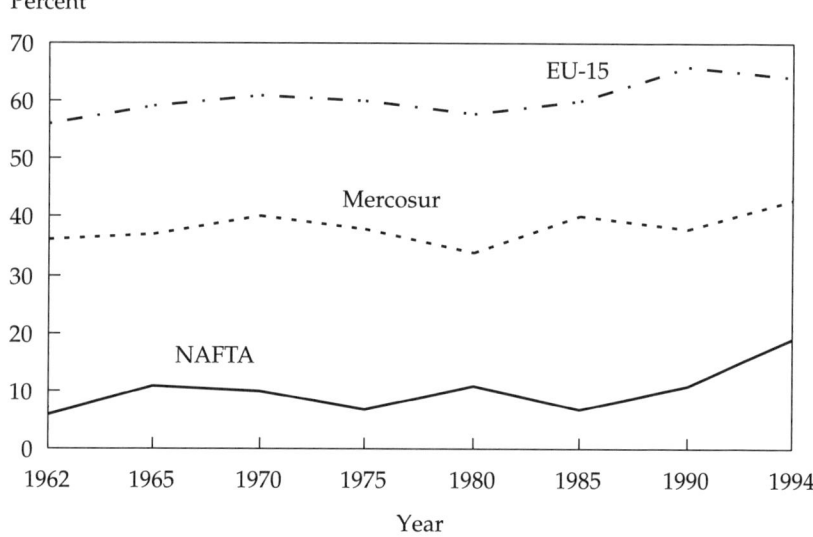

Year

Source: Frankel (1997).

each trade bloc we review the economic and institutional evolution in the region, present an economic profile of the component members, and assess the nature and extent of trade integration.

Chapter 2 surveys trade and transport integration in the NAFTA region comprising Canada, the United States, and Mexico. NAFTA represents the culmination of a long process of trade liberalization that had spawned border-spanning industrial complexes and extensive intra-industrial cross-border trade. Recent reform of the elaborate and divergent economic regulations governing transport in the three countries has conferred economic benefits and has been a prerequisite for the promotion of seamless cross-border goods flow. However, residual economic regulation in the form of cabotage continues to hinder efficient transborder operations. Activities in nontransport matters (such as safety issues, interdiction of drugs, pests, and diseases, and illegal immigration) impose time-intensive inspections. The chapter describes the cooperatve efforts under way to reduce these nontariff barriers to cross-border freight flow in the region.

Chapter 3 addresses the European Union, the oldest and most highly developed of the world's regional trading blocs. Despite more than forty years of history, it is only fairly recently that steps have been taken toward true integration in the transportation sector. Various institutional and technological factors had to be overcome to guarantee true interoperability of infrastructure systems, the seamless movement of goods across international frontiers, and more open markets in transportation systems, including cabotage in freight movements. The chapter stresses the role of supranational institutions—in this case the European Court of Justice and the European Commission—in bringing about greater integration.

Chapter 4 is devoted to Mercosur, the largest trading bloc comprised entirely of developing countries—Argentina, Brazil, Paraguay, and Uruguay with Chile and Bolivia as associate members. Since the creation of Mercosur, there has been a significant and growing interdependence among member economies, with intra-Mercosur trade growing twice as fast as trade with non-Mercosur countries. Efforts are under way to improve the physical and nonphysical infrastructure of transport/trade chains in member countries so that trade growth may continue. This chapter describes some significant efforts at transport service liberalization and deregulation and provides two examples of the benefits of transport integration across Mercosur, as global firms restructure their production and distribution activities in a single market, realizing gains in a virtuous cycle of lower costs, increasing trade, greater economies of scale and scope, and more growth.

Chapter 5 on the Southern African Development Community pays particular attention to the Maputo Corridor. This is a project to create an efficient transportation and communication corridor from the industrial heartland of South Africa to the port of Maputo in Mozambique. The Maputo Corridor exemplifies the development corridors approach, which seeks to expedite international movements of goods and people across international borders while encouraging diversified economic development in infrastructure-rich corridors. Although this project is ongoing, it already is possible to assess some of its achievements.

Chapter 6 focuses on transport and logistics within a South Asia subregion: Bangladesh, Bhutan, Nepal, and eastern India. As the countries position themselves to participate in the global market following recent liberalization policies, they face serious transportation and logistics impediments that have strong implications for economic growth and poverty alleviation in the subregion. The impediments affect the costs of doing business and impair intraregional trade as well as opportunities to participate in international markets. Using detailed logistics cost data, the chapter confirms that the flows of goods traded within the region, especially from landlocked countries, are seriously impaired not only by physical infrastructure bottlenecks but also by policy and procedural impediments in the logistics chain—such as red tape and corruption in customs, delays and pilferage in ports, highly restrictive bilateral protocols on cross-border movement of vehicles, and poor modal interfaces.

Chapter 7 explores how recent globalization trends have affected urban centers in South Asia. In particular, the chapter examines urbanization in the context of evolving trade and transport relations within the South Asia subregion. Using trade patterns among contiguous countries in the subregion, the chapter discusses city performance and competitiveness and provides a peep into the future of the cities.

The final chapter is a case study of Rotterdam, a successful major hub that has maintained its position as the world's largest port for four decades. Rotterdam's ability to retain this preeminent position despite vast changes in the structure of the global economy and the transport sector derives from its twofold approach to trade and transport. First, the port of Rotterdam has marshaled the knowledge and competencies necessary to offer its customers and industrial tenants state-of-the-art services. Second, it has successfully evaluated the larger economic and transportation environment, making in each new era the needed physical, human, and institutional investments. There are clear lessons in Rotterdam's experience for managers of ports and airports in developing countries as they organize their trade-transport chains.

Since the notion of "transport and trade facilitation" (TTF) used here in a trading bloc context is not yet formally developed, we clarify in the next section the cluster of ideas embraced by the term.

Transport and Trade Facilitation

The explosive growth of merchandise trade in many regional trading blocs is a response to the reduction of tariffs and other barriers to intraregional trade. Indeed, the environment for goods flow in recent years has been transformed in affluent industrial countries. Transport is becoming faster, more flexible, and (with jet transport, fast container ships, improved container-handling practices, and intermodal systems) more predictable within a narrow time range. Transport and information industries are being privatized and deregulated. Logistical innovations, such as just-in-time and quick-response services, are reengineering business systems as well as production and commodity flow systems. Containers and cargoes can be tracked around the world by automatic identification devices and are continually "visible" in transit to shippers and carriers. What is more, the slow and tedious paper trail that traditionally has accompanied goods to secure clearances across borders from customs, revenue agencies, and financial intermediaries is being replaced by Electronic Data Interchange (EDI) and e-commerce. Customs agencies, finance ministries, and regulators are beginning to reinvent their practices in this new environment.

The continuity and future growth of trade in Mercosur, or in other trading blocs comprised of developing countries, depend on the efficiency and speed of cross-border transportation of goods, and on the harmonization and simplification of the information processing accompanying those goods. In other words, Mercosur, SAARC, and SADC must move quickly toward the acquisition of the state-of-the-art transport and trade facilitation system noted earlier. The greater the gap between the state-of-the-art TTF system and the system available in a trading bloc, the greater the penalty that specific regional trading bloc will pay in terms of forgone trade and economic growth.

An inadequate trade and transport facilitation system in Mercosur, or in any other regional trading bloc, creates an efficiency penalty. International agencies estimate that antiquated types of trade administration and the failure to adopt IT-supported trade facilitation (and the downstream effects of those systems) account for 7 percent of the value of the goods (Schware and Kimberley, 1995).

If developing countries in Mercosur or in the free trade areas in South Asia and South Africa have substandard TTF systems, they cannot participate effectively in the global production networks. As noted earlier, the increasing division of labor in the global economy leads to a partition of the production "value chain" among production locales that are spatially distributed in many countries. One third of world trade in the mid-1990s occurred within global production networks (World Bank, 2000b).

Manufacturing industries continue to be reallocated in these networks from industrial countries to developing regions. Therefore, trade expansion is likely, not only in goods but also in services. Unimproved transport and trade facilitation systems can reduce trade and thereby restrict the benefits of globalization—expanded markets for exports, the acquisition of new technology, and the favorable effect of competition on the efficiency of domestic producers.

The long-term benefits of a superior TTF system lie beyond the cost-reduction and trade expansion benefits already noted. There is great potential for cross-border integration of manufacturing and service activities and for exploiting the economies of scope and scale in the larger market. In time, self-sustaining economic expansion results. Although such developments take time, they can set in motion a sequence of cumulative processes that lead from falling costs to output increases to incentives for the creation of spatial agglomerations of production (cities) to rising output and profits, in turn attracting more production to these cities.

The Components of an Advanced TTF System

An advanced trade and transport facilitation system (table 1-1) reduces the barriers to transport and cross-border transit in two ways: through *physical infrastructure* (transport infrastructure and facilities, and communication infrastructure that complements transport infrastructure) and *nonphysical infrastructure* (knowledge and competencies applied to the physical infrastructure). The latter include knowledge about how to transport and communicate in specific legal, economic, financial, and political frameworks and how such frameworks can improve transport and trade.

Physical Infrastructure

The physical infrastructure of an advanced TTF system has transport components as well as information components. Both will be discussed in this section. An effective intermodal transport system will reduce the physical constraints of potentially cost-effective corridors linking neighboring countries. Effective corridors and efficient intermodal facilities are abundant in the NAFTA countries and in the European Union, but numerous barriers to cross-border movement exist in Mercosur and in the SAARC and SADC regions. These constraints include physical bottlenecks on road networks (for example, missing links, absence of ferry crossings, and narrow and unsturdy bridges); poor maintenance; multiple gauges in the rail system; inadequate dredging, poor lighting, and bad positioning of navigation aids in inland waterways; and inadequate transshipment/storage and container facilities at cross-border stations.

Table 1-1. Components of an Advanced Transport and Trade Facilitation System

Physical infrastructure
    Transport subsystems
    Information subsystems

Nonphysical infrastructure (knowledge and competencies in transport and trade facilitation)
    Overall governance of transport and trade facilitation
    Business logistical systems
    Financial coordination
    Governance of physical flows

Source: The author developed this classification.

Developing countries often lack investment in *micro-infrastructure* (for example, poorly developed physical facilities for parking, handling, and storage at customs areas in border crossings). These inadequacies lead to costly delays in customs clearance. Investments in railway modernization, highway improvements, upgrading of ports and inland waterways and airports, and intermodal coordination should address these transportation infrastructure deficiencies.

Information technologies now make possible the rapid collection, transfer, and analysis of "intelligence" associated with the merchandise being traded. This accelerated information processing and information exchange promotes preclearance and prereconciliation at various stages of trading transactions. Costs are much lower than those of the traditional paper systems, and incompatibilities of technology, time, and distance are more easily resolved. Information is exchanged between computers by Electronic Data Interchange.

The EDI associated with international transport substitutes the legal transmission of electronic information in the customs process for paper inputs—leading to major savings in time and money. Implementation is done using the UN/EDIFACT document standard. The Internet and electronic commerce services can play an important role in a reengineered trade facilitation process within countries and across borders.

Nonphysical Infrastructure

Four aspects of the nonphysical infrastructure in an advanced trade and transport facilitation system are noteworthy: overall governance of transport and trade facilitation, new logistical systems for businesses, financial coordination, and physical flows. Each will be examined in turn. Efficient cross-border movement of cargo requires legal, institutional, regulatory, and administrative innovations. Examples include:

- Deregulation of transport services
- Removal of cabotage and other residual economic regulations
- Privatization of transport infrastructure
- Reform of the commercial legal framework
- Reinvention of the customs function
- Adoption of international standards and trade practices.

Business capabilities are enhanced by new logistical systems that offer fast, reliable, and low-cost service. These systems also can provide competitive advantage by slashing costs (minimum inventory), quickening market feedback, and expanding market reach.

Financial coordination is improved by trade-friendly banking practices and new payment systems. Risk-reduction innovations can reduce the costs of linking the shipper and the customer. Organizational innovations can create efficient entities for marketing and distribution in the rapidly evolving global marketplace (box 1-1).

Finally, an advanced trade and transport facilitation system governs physical flows. Knowledge and competencies in TTF can harmonize the size and weight of cross-border vehicles, promote seamless intermodal freight flows across borders, reengineer inspection activities, and lessen delays in noncustoms inspections.

Lessons Learned

The following chapters present case studies on the NAFTA countries, the European Union, Mercosur, the Southern African Development Community, and the South Asia subregion. From these studies of regional trading blocs important lessons can be learned.

First, a regional trading bloc with a high level of economic integration and high volumes of trade cannot be achieved as the result of a single free trade agreement. Even North America and Europe, highly industrialized regions with a long history of open trade, did not attain such an outcome in one fell swoop. Rather, economic integration has evolved, as in NAFTA, over several decades, largely because of policies that have promoted development of border-spanning industrial complexes resulting in intra-industry trade of high-value goods. In the case of Canada and the United States, free trade was promoted initially by a sectoral trade agreement (the Auto Pact of 1965) and later, in 1988, by the Canada-U.S. Free Trade Agreement. In the case of Mexico and the United States, policies by both governments facilitated, over time, free trade in the border areas (the Maquiladora system).

Similarly, trade today between the fifteen members of the European Union is the result of slow and steady progress. The European Union's high level of integration (not only in trade but also in labor market, monetary, social, and environmental policy areas) has evolved over four decades—from the humble beginnings of the 1951 European Coal and Steel Community (ECSC) to the Treaty of Rome (1960) and the Mastricht Treaty (1992). These agreements have eliminated some of the remaining trade barriers and created opportunities to expand well-established trade relationships.

In the case of developing countries that band together to form a regional trading bloc, there is a further history-induced frictional factor. As a consequence of past semicolonial trade links to Europe and North America, Mercosur member countries have had stronger trade and financial links with European and North American economies than with one another: intraregional trade in this part of the world has been a small

Box 1-1. Best-Practice Trade and Transport Logistics

In recent years cross-border trade has grown enormously, and international business-to-business transactions via the Internet have increased rapidly. In response, a variety of innovations have appeared to improve the efficiency of the supply chain worldwide and to harmonize foreign trade rules and regulations as well as payment issues. In order to be more responsive to their customers, the developers of these logistical systems in the United States are developing strategic partnerships with their client businesses. Closer collaboration between the users and developers of logistical software has had several benefits.

Global Positioning Satellite (GPS) technology is transforming the effectiveness of current transportation services. New systems blend three existing capabilities: planning and scheduling logistics software, in-cab communication systems for scheduling and monitoring trucks, and electronic links between the firm developing logistics systems and the retailer supply chain. GPS technology can help businesses monitor the location of trucks and dispatch them to ensure faster delivery and better stock of merchandise at the retailers' shops.

Comprehensive systems can manage the entire supply chain, in the process blurring the distinction between production, transport, and distribution activities. Sowinski (2000) describes new logistical software that brings together diverse information on raw materials, input suppliers, factories, transport vehicles, and points-of-sale in real time. These information and analytical systems can help businesses (1) make decisions on how many warehouses or plants to build and where, and what modes of transport to use; and (2) compute tradeoffs between production run length and inventory costs, thus making it easier to assess when to open or close production lines.

New logistical systems that can support efficient cross-border supply chains offer information not only on transport, insurance, and other costs, but also on cross-border transit of goods. A New York firm offers clients information via the World Wide Web—a low-cost source of access to pertinent export regulation information. The resulting Automated Export System (AES) is certified by the U.S. Customs Service and the Foreign Trade Division of the U.S. Census Bureau to permit electronic filing of export documentation used by exporters and freight forwarders. Other systems supply exporters with more than 700 international trade documents in 21 languages and a variety of international banking requirements for trade activities. They help small and medium enterprises lower the time and cost of cross-border trade and transport.

Source: Sowinski (2000).

share of total trade. Inward-looking trade regimes and import substitution development strategies during the past three or four decades weakened intraregional economic links.

In the case of South Asia, partition of the Indian subcontinent in the postcolonial era into a number of countries has, over time, severed or restricted transport movements along traditional transport corridors (for example, the Calcutta-Bangladesh-Assam corridor). In addition to the trade and transport facilitation policies noted in this book, special efforts are needed to overcome historical intraregional transport frictions within Mercosur and in Southern Africa and South Asia. Such efforts in the developing-country trading blocs will modify earlier orientations and promote the exploitation of new economic complementarities among these countries. The benefits of proximity and lower transport costs can then be enjoyed. Over time, such developments will stimulate trade creation, rationalization of economic activities within the entire bloc, and overall expansion.

Real progress toward fuller economic integration may require strong supranational institutions. Although the European Union has eliminated border checks and achieved full cabotage in some service categories, member countries clung for years to the status quo of fragmented transport infrastructure and regulation. Government ownership of major transport carriers and the role of transport policy in advancing national economic goals are two reasons for this resistance to change. A supranational institution, the European Court of Justice, played a critical role in breaking down the national prerogatives that had prevented a Common Transport Policy within the European Union for thirty years. In the case of air transportation, the European Commission advocated regulatory reform that was opposed by all member states in 1979. After almost a decade of debate and litigation, regulatory reform was implemented.

Before the signing of the North American Free Trade Agreement in 1994, the member countries engaged in preparatory work that included extensive economic deregulation of the transport sector and privatization. Customs practices were reformed as well. The recent acceleration of transport integration in EU countries reflects similar reforms of the legal, regulatory, and administrative aspects of the transport sector. It is imperative for Mercosur countries, and for the South Asian and Southern African regions, to engage in similar reforms. Only then can developing-country trading blocs acquire favorable access to global production networks where so much value is being created.

2

Transport and Trade in the North American Free Trade Agreement

T. R. Lakshmanan and William P. Anderson

The North American Free Trade Agreement (NAFTA), signed on January 1, 1994, created the largest trading bloc in the world. By abolishing all tariffs over a ten-year period, and by eliminating certain administrative nontariff barriers such as import licenses and local content rules, NAFTA was designed to open the borders separating Canada, Mexico, and the United States to the free exchange of goods and services.

NAFTA represents the culmination of a long process of trade liberalization. In the pre-NAFTA era, there was tariff free movement of goods within a specific sector between Canada and the United States, and within designated zones between Mexico and the United States. Consonant and complementary policies in transportation deregulation and privatization in the same period also helped to lower trade barriers. The result was development of border-spanning industrial complexes producing large volumes of trade in high value-added manufactured goods. By removing most of the remaining barriers to cross-border goods movement, NAFTA provides opportunities to expand and extend trade relationships that were already well established at the time of its implementation.

Despite the comprehensive nature of NAFTA and the favorable history that led up to it, trade within this area is not completely "free" in the sense that cross-border movement of goods is no more costly than the movement of the same goods over the same distance within a country. If this is not the case, then internationally traded goods will be at some competitive disadvantage to domestically traded goods. Despite NAFTA, there are still a number of factors that may hinder the free movement of goods across borders and therefore the full potential of free trade may not be realized.

Such factors embraced by the term *nontariff barriers* include:

1. the threat of illegal movements of undocumented people, drugs, and materials that may transport pests or disease, resulting in the need for time-consuming inspections at borders;
2. inconsistency in technical and safety-related transportation regulations such as vehicle size and weight restrictions; and
3. residual economic regulations as related to cabotage and restrictions on certain product movements.

The focus of this chapter is on the remaining barriers in the NAFTA transport and transit facilitation system. Thus, our concern is with the second and third categories, which prevent the seamless integration of national transportation systems, and to a limited extent the first category, which can result in impediments to the movement of goods. We will identify transportation factors that act as barriers to trade, explain and assess their current situation, and describe measures that are being taken to mitigate their impacts.

While the chapter addresses issues involving the broader freight transportation sector, it places particular emphasis on trucking, the dominant mode of freight transportation in North America. In the United States trucking accounts for more than 70 percent of the goods moved by value and more than 50 percent by weight (U.S. Department of Transportation, 1997b, table 9-5). As the next section of the chapter will show, trade across the U.S.-Canada and U.S.-Mexico borders is mostly in relatively high value manufactured goods and components, a market segment in which trucking is even more dominant. Furthermore, some of the most important problems involved in cross-border transportation integration arise in the trucking mode.

The chapter begins with an economic overview of the NAFTA partners and existing trade relationships and a review of some of the main provisions of the agreement. We then discuss three major issues related to transportation and trade: economic regulation, technical regulation, and border crossings. The chapter concludes with lessons learned from the NAFTA experience that can be applied to other free trade areas.

NAFTA: The Scope and Evolution of Trade Integration

The three NAFTA partners are a diverse group in terms of size, level of development, and the role of trade in their economies. While Canada and the United States both rank among the highest income countries in the world, Canada is dwarfed by the United States in terms of population and GNP (table 2-1). International trade is more critical to the Canadian economy, as indicated by the ratio of total trade to GDP. Thus, the

Table 2-1. Statistical Comparison of the NAFTA Countries, Selected Years, 1990–98

Indicator	Canada	Mexico	U.S.
GNP, 1998 (billions of U.S. dollars)	612.2	380.9	7,921.3
Average GNP growth rate, 1990–98	2.2	2.5	2.9
GNP per capita, 1998 (U.S. dollars)[a]	24,050	8,190	29,340
Total trade as percentage of GDP, 1996	73	42	24
Population, 1998 (millions)	31	96	270
Average percentage population growth, 1990–98	1.4	2.0	1.1

a. Adjusted for purchasing power parity.
Source: World Bank (2000b).

United States and Canada roughly fit the classic "large country/small country" case of international trade theory. Mexico is a relatively low-income country that has been experiencing rapid economic growth in recent years. Given its large population, rapid economic growth, and opportunities for economic integration with its richer neighbors, Mexico could be one of the most important international markets in the twenty-first century. Figure 2-1 traces the growth of the three economies in the 1993–97 period and the growing importance of trade in all the economies.

Canada and the United States now have the largest bilateral trade relationship in the world, but this was not always the case. Between the time the United States became an independent country in 1776 and the mid-nineteenth century, the U.S.-Canadian Colony commercial relations were strained. After a short thaw between 1846 (when Britain adopted a policy of free trade) and the American Civil War (when Britain was suspected of helping the southern states), U.S.-Canadian trade was open and unrestrained. After the Civil War, the United States abrogated this free trade regime unilaterally. Later, in 1879, the then-autonomous Canadian Government instituted a policy of tariff barriers—partly to protect its nascent manufacturing industries (against a more robust U.S. production sector) and partly to unify a geographically vast country by diverting North-South international trade flows to East-West domestic trade. Over time this policy led to an expansion of interprovincial trade, large and efficient industries (steel, agricultural machinery, and other key sectors), and a "branch plant" economy with U.S. interests owning half or more of Canadian manufacturing capacity.

Tariff barriers have declined over time, due partly to the General Agreement on Tariffs and Trade (GATT) but more significantly to the U.S.-Canada Auto Pact of 1965. This was an agreement to eliminate all tariffs

Figure 2-1. GNP and Trade as a Percentage of GDP in Canada, Mexico, and the United States, 1993 and 1997

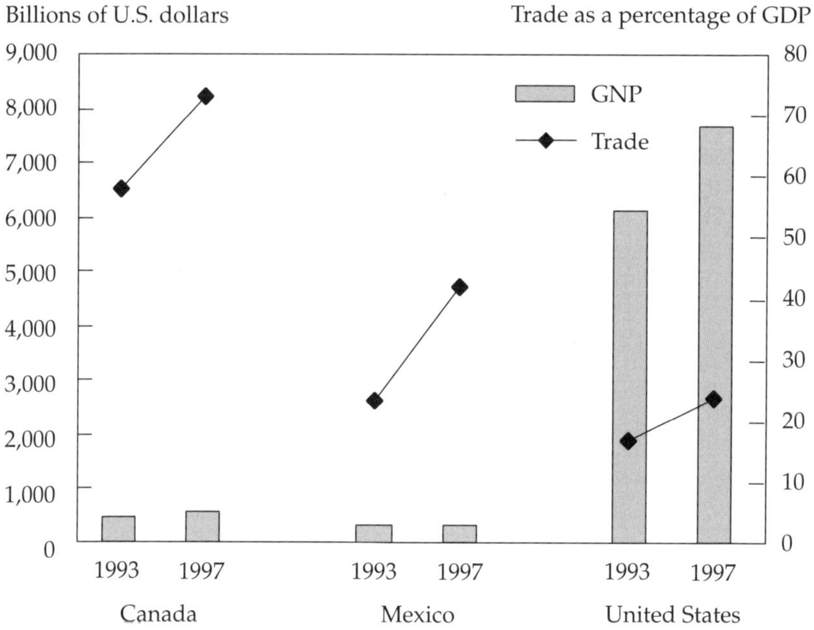

Billions of U.S. dollars   Trade as a percentage of GDP

Source: Data are from World Bank (2000b).

on automotive products and components, thus allowing Ford, Chrysler, and General Motors to rationalize their North American production system. The agreement included provisions to ensure an equitable market share for Canadian production plants. The importance of this Auto Pact in shaping U.S.-Canada trade relations is evident in the fact that automotive products now dominate U.S.-Canada trade. More generally, a trade regime in which intra-industry trade and trade in intermediate goods play prominent roles emerged as a result of that agreement.

More comprehensive trade liberalization was achieved under another NAFTA precursor, the Canada-U.S. Free Trade Agreement of 1988 (CUSFTA), which was intended to phase out by 1998 all Canada-U.S. tariffs. While CUSFTA served as a model for the removal of barriers to trade in services, transportation services were not covered under CUSFTA because the United States was still implementing a broad program of transportation deregulation and Canada was just beginning a similar program at the time under this agreement.

Even before CUSFTA, Canada's international trade was dominated by its relationship with the United States. By 1998, the United States was the destination of 84 percent of Canada's exports (by value) and the origin of 77 percent of Canada's imports. This fact, coupled with Canada's high ratio of trade to GDP, indicate the extraordinary degree to which the Canadian economy is dependent upon the U.S. economy.

Table 2-2 breaks out Canada-U.S. trade by broad commodity groups, revealing a trade pattern quite different from the pattern in the late nineteenth and early twentieth centuries, when Canada exported primary commodities and its industrial sector was poorly developed. At present more than 70 percent of Canada's exports to the United States are manufactured goods, of which most are machinery and transportation equipment coming largely from the industrial provinces of Ontario and Quebec.

U.S.-Mexican relations are based on shaky historical foundations. Mexico lost roughly half of its territories (including California) to the United States as the outcome of a war fought between the two countries in the 1840s. Subsequent U.S. intervention (sometimes of a military nature) in Mexican affairs led a succession of Mexican governments to be highly suspicious of their northern neighbor. Nevertheless, the Mexican economy is highly dependent on the United States, not only because of the size of the American market, but also because the American earnings of Mexican emigrants—both permanent and temporary—contribute significantly to Mexico's aggregate income.

The most important pre-NAFTA development in Mexico-U.S. trade relations has been the creation of "Maquiladora" assembly plants. Located in Mexico, these plants use mostly U.S. components and produce almost exclusively for the U.S. market. They permit American manufacturers to use low-wage Mexican labor in the assembly phases of production that require relatively low skill levels.

Under the customs provisions enacted by the U.S. and Mexican governments, Mexico allows U.S. components to enter duty-free and be held in-bond at the Maquiladora site, so long as the finished products are re-exported. Upon shipment from the Maquiladora, U.S. customs charge duty only on the Mexican value-added content of the assembled product.

From the Mexican perspective, this system generates employment and income. From the U.S. perspective, it makes U.S. producers more competitive while preserving jobs in component manufacturing. Thus, despite the absence of any formal treaty, complementary U.S. and Mexican policy measures have created a mutually beneficial trade relationship.

Due in large part to this system of production, exports from Mexico are primarily in the manufacturing categories (table 2-3). Despite the

Table 2-2. U.S. Trade with Canada, 1993 and 1997

	1993		1997	
U.S. exports	Millions of dollars	Percent	Millions of dollars	Percent
Food and live animals	5,573	5.5	6,879	4.5
Beverages and tobacco	148	0.1	320	0.2
Crude materials, inedible, except fuels	3,144	3.1	4,453	3.0
Mineral, fuels, lubricants, and related materials	1,257	1.2	2,420	1.6
Animal and vegetable oils, fats, waxes	89	0.1	229	0.1
Chemical and related products N.E.S.	8,419	8.4	13,093	8.7
Manufactured goods classified chiefly by material	12,431	12.4	19,652	13.1
Machinery and transport equipment	54,273	54.2	82,961	55.3
Miscellaneous manufactured articles	10,458	10.4	14,773	9.8
Other	4,397	4.4	5,344	3.6
Total	100,190	100.0	150,124	100.0

	1993		1997	
U.S. imports	Millions of dollars	Percent	Millions of dollars	Percent
Food and live animals	4,899	4.4	7,434	4.4
Beverages and tobacco	1,138	1.0	823	0.5
Crude materials, inedible, except fuels	8,417	7.6	11,983	7.1
Mineral, fuels, lubricants, and related materials	11,772	10.6	17,908	10.7
Animal and vegetable oils, fats, waxes	219	0.2	379	0.2
Chemical and related products N.E.S.	5,499	5.0	9,514	5.7
Manufactured goods classified chiefly by material	17,765	16.0	27,336	16.3
Machinery and transport equipment	48,999	44.1	72,101	42.9
Miscellaneous manufactured articles	5,255	4.7	10,306	6.1
Other	6,958	6.3	10,266	6.1
Total	110,921	100.0	168,051	100.0

Source: U.S. Department of Commerce (various years).

extreme economic differences between Canada and Mexico, the U.S.-Canada and U.S.-Mexico trade profiles are relatively similar. Both are dominated by intra-industry trade of manufactured goods arising from a high degree of integration with U.S. production systems. There is a fundamental difference, however, between these two bilateral trade re-

Table 2-3. U.S. Trade with Mexico, 1993 and 1997

U.S. exports	1993		1997	
	Millions of dollars	Percent	Millions of dollars	Percent
Food and live animals	2,460	5.9	3,074	4.3
Beverages and tobacco	150	0.4	82	0.1
Crude materials, inedible, except fuels	1,808	4.3	2,956	4.1
Mineral, fuels, lubricants, and related materials	1,044	2.5	2,006	2.8
Animal and vegetable oils, fats, waxes	212	0.5	375	0.5
Chemical and related products N.E.S.	3,470	8.3	6,343	8.9
Manufactured goods classified chiefly by material	5,529	13.3	9,319	13.1
Machinery and transport equipment	19,760	47.5	35,810	50.2
Miscellaneous manufactured articles	5,361	12.9	8,394	11.8
Other	1,843	4.4	3,019	4.2
Total	41,635	100.0	71,378	100.0

U.S. imports	1993		1997	
	Millions of dollars	Percent	Millions of dollars	Percent
Food and live animals	2,680	6.7	3,917	4.6
Beverages and tobacco	320	0.8	704	0.8
Crude materials, inedible, except fuels	652	1.6	978	1.1
Mineral, fuels, lubricants, and related materials	4,869	12.2	8,449	9.8
Animal and vegetable oils, fats, waxes	27	0.0	29	0.0
Chemical and related products N.E.S.	772	1.9	1,551	1.8
Manufactured goods classified chiefly by material	2,903	7.3	6,642	7.7
Machinery and transport equipment	20,732	51.9	47,312	55.1
Miscellaneous manufactured articles	5,245	13.1	12,953	15.1
Other	1,730	4.3	3,337	3.9
Total	39,930	100.0	85,872	100.0

Source: U.S. Department of Commerce (various years).

lationships. U.S.-Canada trade is between two highly developed countries and is therefore comparable to the intra-industry trade between members of the European Community (EC). By contrast, economic integration between the United States and Mexico is of a specific form dictated by the large differences in wage and skills levels between the two countries.

In assessing the potential and progress of NAFTA, it is important to keep in mind trade history. NAFTA was introduced at a time when a particular form of trade involving industrial complexes that span the borders between the United States and its two neighbors had already evolved over a period of decades. (Trade between Canada and Mexico is still very small.) Thus NAFTA creates an opportunity to expand and extend trade relationships that are already well established.

Overview of NAFTA

NAFTA is a highly comprehensive trade area agreement. It covers not only tariff elimination but also a number of highly contentious issues, including nontariff barriers, direct foreign investment, trade and services, government procurement, and intellectual property rights. Despite its broad scope, the agreement contains a variety of exceptions and safeguard measures. One of the most important aspects of NAFTA is its provisions for dispute resolution.

Tariff Elimination. NAFTA requires all tariffs on industrial goods to be eliminated within ten years of its implementation date (that is, by 2004). A few Mexican tariffs on agricultural goods will be eliminated over a fifteen-year period.

Since NAFTA does not impose common external tariffs, transparent rules of origin prevent any fourth country from reducing tariff burdens by exporting to one NAFTA partner and then re-exporting to another partner with a higher external tariff. NAFTA content rules prevent transshipment of goods after only minor processing. Despite the basic principle that all tariffs should be eliminated, safeguard provisions allow any NAFTA partner to reinstate its tariffs if imports cause serious injury to a domestic industry.

Nontariff Barriers. Administrative nontariff barriers, such as the issuing of import licenses that can effectively act as quotas, are eliminated under NAFTA. While accepting that technical product standards may vary across countries, NAFTA stipulates that they not be used as obstacles to trade. Specific provisions include the right of firms in one country to participate in the standard-setting procedures of another and appointment of a committee to promote the harmonization of standards.

Trade in Services. NAFTA allows free trade in the majority of service sectors. Major exclusions include marine and air transportation and basic telecommunications. The fact that services are "covered" under NAFTA does not mean that all restrictions to trade have been eliminated.

For example, as we explain later in this chapter, the definition of land transportation as a tradable service under NAFTA does not mean that all restrictions to cross-border truck and rail operation have been removed.

Investment. Under NAFTA, foreign and domestic investors have the same rights in most cases. Certain sectors are exempt, including maritime and telecommunications, and each country may prohibit foreign investment in specific activities based on national security. Because of provisions in the Mexican constitution, the energy sector and railroads are exempt in that country.

Government Procurement. NAFTA significantly expands the opportunities for firms in one country to bid on government contracts in another. Significantly, Mexico's state-controlled industries (oil and gas, electricity) are opened up to foreign procurement. A variety of restrictions, such as small and minority business set-asides in U.S. government contracts, remain.

Personnel. NAFTA does not provide for free movement of labor across borders. It does, however, make it easier for businesspeople to move between countries, so long as it is on a temporary basis.

Dispute Resolution. One of the most important features of NAFTA is the establishment of fair, transparent, and timely resolution of disputes. NAFTA panels can be convened to settle disagreements concerning the application of rules of origin, NAFTA content rules, or the application of antidumping measures. NAFTA panels also have authority over disputes related to environmental practices in border areas.

Transportation and Trade Facilitation under NAFTA

Under NAFTA, the production and transportation firms in the United States, Canada, and Mexico have begun to rationalize their production and logistical systems to suit a single North American market. This drive for rationalization and increasing trade have generated, in turn, demand for more economic harmonization and fewer obstacles to free trade. Some aspects of transportation, however, still impede free trade.

In transportation NAFTA sought to make U.S.-Mexico transborder operations comparable to U.S.-Canada operations. Reciprocal entry in the trucking industry was to be permitted until December 1995 to zones in border states, later to border states, and by 2000 to all states and all over Mexico. Yet more than half a decade into NAFTA, in transborder traffic there remain many subtle and not so subtle barriers that translate into higher costs. Why is this so given the convergence since the 1970s in economic regulation and the liberalized environment for transport in the three countries—particularly between the United States and Canada where the business practices are similar and the infrastructures are compatible?

It is worth noting that the three countries have domestic transportation systems that reflect their differing public policy and regulatory regimes. The technical and safety-related regulations (for example, vehicle size and weight standards) that have developed in each country over the years to govern domestic transportation are divergent enough to provide barriers to transborder traffic. Many of these standards are complex and multidimensional. To resolve inconsistencies requires considerable effort. The work of the Land Transportation Standards Subcommittee (LTSS) is a case in point.

Reform of the elaborate and divergent economic regulations governing transport in the three countries has been a prerequisite for the promotion of a seamless cross-border freight flow. In North America, transport deregulation and privatization have complemented trade liberalization in an effort to promote transport integration. Despite the economic regulatory reform that has occurred in Canada, Mexico, and the United States, economic regulation in the form of cabotage rules continues to hinder efficient transborder operations. Activities in nontransport matters (such as interdiction of drugs, pests, and diseases, and illegal immigration) lead to time-consuming border inspections.

The rest of the chapter explores these nontariff barriers. It details their nature and complexity, their current status, and the steps that are being taken to lower nontariff barriers and mitigate their effects.

Economic Deregulation: Prerequisite for Seamless Cross-Border Transportation

The public policy regimes in transport in North America have included a high level of economic regulation for nearly a century. Transportation carriers, which are integrated with fixed facilities and vehicles and enjoy network economies, were able to engage in monopoly pricing, market segmentation pricing, and similar actions that seriously disadvantaged shippers and communities.

Since 1887, when the Interstate Commerce Commission (ICC) was created, the United States has regulated railroads to ensure a normal rate of return to them on their assets while balancing the advantages of shippers and equity of service to communities. To this end the ICC engaged in elaborate control of investment, pricing, and operations in the railroad industry. It specified the conditions of entry and exit, and it created a complex rate structure, and even rules of operations. During the 1930s similar economic regulation was extended to motor carriers and airlines. Canadian carriers have also been subject to economic regulation, though more lightly than U.S. carriers and predominantly at the provincial level. Mexico also regulated through the award of transport concessions, the grant of route capacity, and freight rate structures.

By the 1970s the adverse effects of such intrusive regulation had become very evident in the poor financial performance of U.S. railroads and high truck rates in the LTL (less than truckload) sector. Economic analyses have shown that price and entry regulations introduce inefficiency by creating a vicious cycle of artificially high prices, high service quality competition, and the resultant losses due to raised costs (Douglas and Miller, 1974). Three sets of such regulatory distortions have proved costly. First, in both road and rail, rates were set above marginal costs—costing the economy $1 billion annually (Winston, 1985). Second, the entry and exit regulations cost the carriers dearly: the prohibition on railroads exiting from poorly performing lines led to annual production cost inefficiencies of $2.5 billion (Winston, 1985). Third, restrictions such as disallowing backhauls and designation of routes led to X-inefficiency costs of several billion dollars (Winston, Corsi, and Grimm, 1990). The restrictions also hindered productivity growth, technical change, and improvement of service quality.

The resulting drive for deregulation led in short order to regulatory reform in the United States of airlines (1978), railroads (1980), and motor carriers (1980). Entry conditions were eased; freedom to price was promoted; reliance on the market and competition were encouraged. Canada followed suit with passage of the National Transportation Act of 1987 (NTA), the Shipping Conferences Exemption Act (SCEA), the Motor Vehicle Transport Act, and amendments to other legislation such as the Railway Act.

In Mexico transport was deregulated in the late 1980s as part of an economic restructuring intended to promote domestic investment-friendly policies. Liberalization of the motor carrier industry occurred in 1989. This permitted greater pricing freedom, opened the market to private carriers, and allowed Maquiladora operators to use their own fleets to move goods in both directions.

Major changes occurred in the United States in the conduct, performance, and structure of airlines, trucking, and railroads after deregulation—more competition among all modal carriers, lower prices, wider service offerings, and new entry into most geographic and product markets (figures 2-2 and 2-3). Carriers have been able to rationalize their networks, improve the efficiency of their operations, and set rates in line with competitive market conditions. There was a significant change in

Figure 2-2. Operating Costs of Less-than-Truckload and Truckload Carriers, Selected Years, 1977–95

Costs in 1995 dollars per vehicle mile

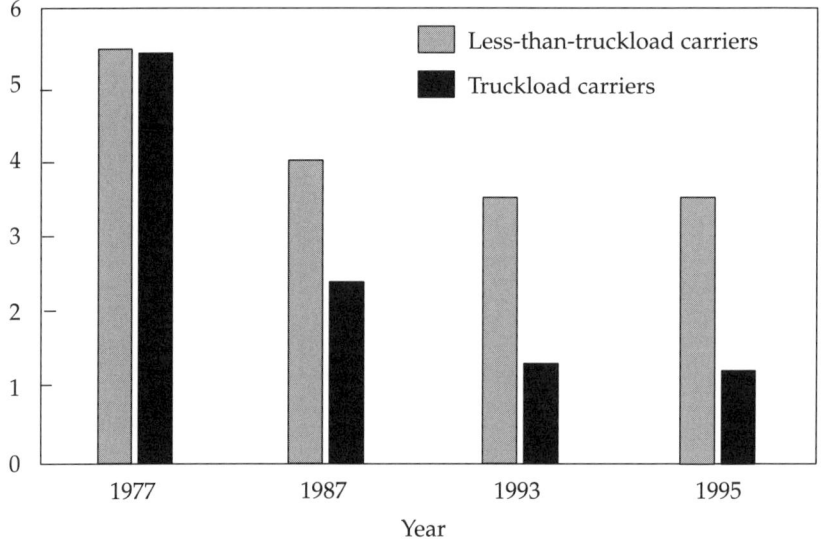

Source: Morrison and Winston (1999).

the cost structure of the railroad industry following deregulation, with productivity growing at well over 2 percent a year (Bereskin, 1996).

Several studies have shown that average airfares (in constant dollars) have fallen since 1978, and competition stays rigorous on most city-pair routes, though concentration has gone up in the industry (U.S. General Accounting Office, 1990; NRC, 1991). U.S. domestic airfares adjusted for distance have been consistently lower in the past two decades than in Europe, Asia, or the world (figure 2-4).

Shippers, confronting technological change and globalization, have begun to coordinate their production activities more effectively with their transportation services. Productivity gains have resulted. The experience in Canada since 1987 has been broadly similar, with competitive pressures lowering rates in international air traffic, railroads, and trucking (figure 2-5.) Trucking deregulation in Mexico in 1989 increased competition and lowered rates—29 percent lower a few years later (Strah, 1995). It also promoted expansion of intercity routes and the vehicle fleet.

Figure 2-3. Railroad Operating Costs per Revenue Ton-Mile, 1980–95

Costs in 1995 dollars per ton-mile

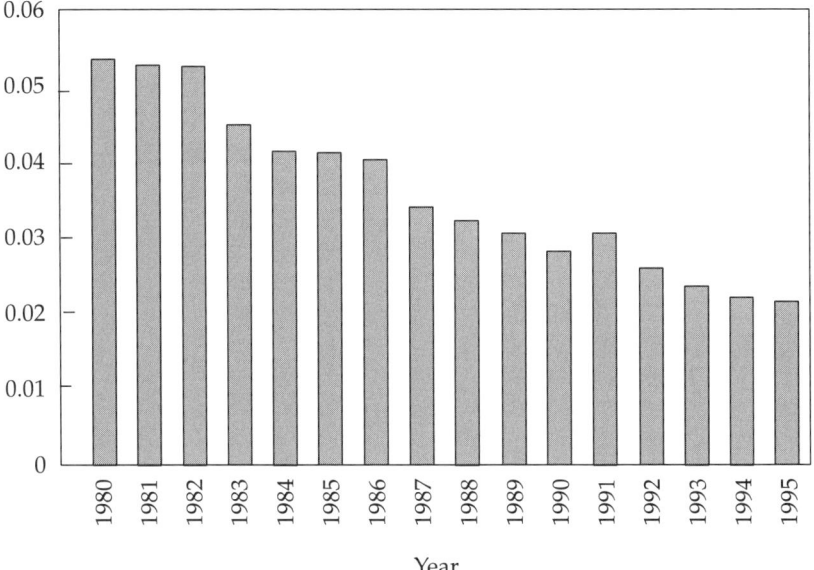

Year

Source: Morrison and Winston (1999).

One class of these barriers pertains to the remaining economic regulation, in particular, *cabotage*. Cabotage refers to the ability of foreign vehicles and labor to transport goods within a country. The cabotage rules and regulations that limit the freedom of foreign transportation carriers instituted by customs and immigration departments are typically symmetric. Such rules involve the use of labor and equipment of one country in the other. For example, foreign drivers cannot carry domestic freight, and the use of foreign equipment is restricted to domestic movements that are incidental to international movements. The existence of these cabotage-rule barriers increases the cost of transborder transport. Railroads are less affected by cabotage restrictions, though they, too, incur additional costs because of the need to change crews at the border.

U.S. restrictions on trade in domestic water transportation represent another cabotage barrier. In the large, multicoastal U.S. economy, foreign participation in its intercoastal trade is restricted by the 1920 Jones Act. The Jones Act—justified by the need to secure a sufficient merchant

Figure 2-4. Difference between International Fares (U.S.-Foreign) and U.S. Domestic Fares Adjusted for Distance, Selected Years, 1978–96

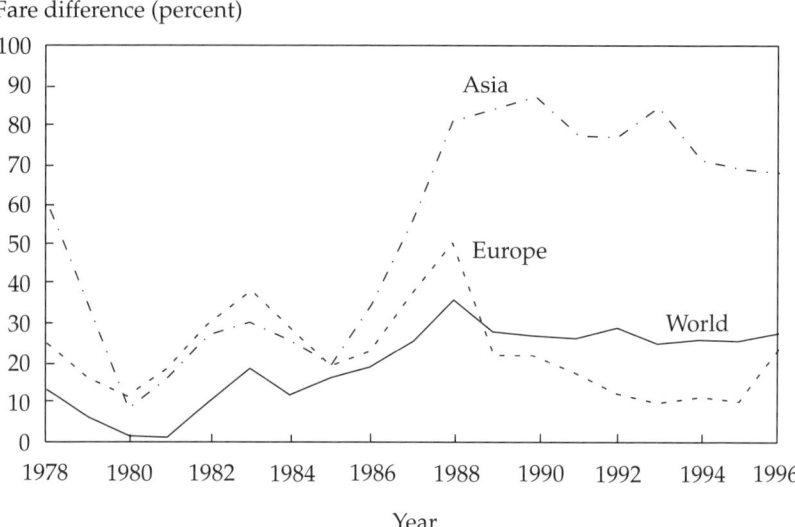

Fare difference (percent)

Source: Morrison and Winston (1999).

marine capacity for U.S. defense needs—reserves the shipping cabotage traffic to U.S.-built and registered ships that are predominantly owned and crewed by U.S. nationals. The U.S. maritime carriers and other stakeholders have excluded these provisions from the GATT and NAFTA. The Jones Act permits domestic shippers to levy rates substantially above comparable world prices, effecting thereby a massive transfer from U.S. users of water transport to U.S. maritime carriers—a welfare cost around $3 billion in 1989 according to an analysis of the Jones Act (Francois and others, 1996).

Aviation is an important component of foreign trade. In 1995 it accounted for $355 billion or 27 percent of U.S. trade—60 percent of which is hauled in U.S. carriers (U.S. General Accounting Office, 1996). The rapid growth in international air freight services reflects the emergence of global systems of producing and distributing goods and the associated "just-in-time" inventory and supply chain management systems. Such services are handicapped, however, by the bilateral international aviation agreements that specify traffic rights—the routes, the number

Figure 2-5. Canadian Railroad Costs, 1980–91

Costs in 1986 cents per revenue ton-mile

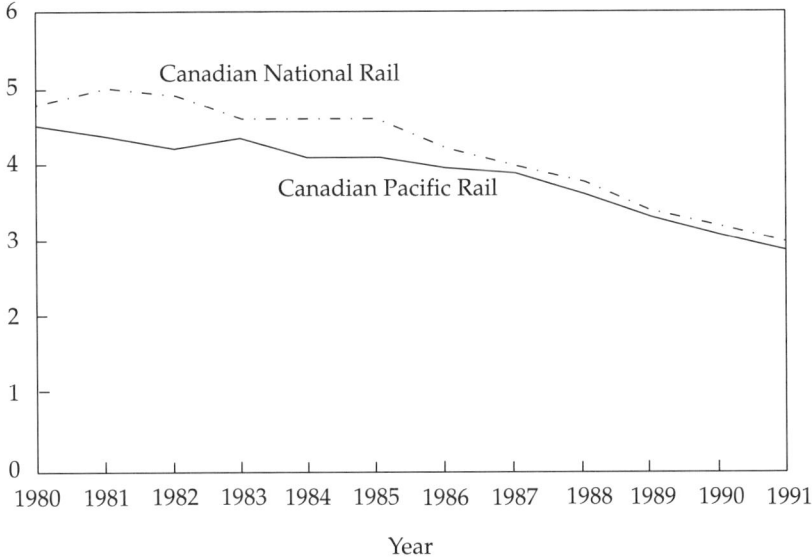

Year

Source: IBI, Consulting.

of flights on each route, and the number of airlines that can fly them. "Open skies" agreements recently negotiated by the United States with European countries, such as Germany and the Netherlands, have relaxed such restrictions on transborder airline traffic. In 1995 the United States and Canada signed the Open Skies Agreement under which carriers in each country were given full access to destinations in the other, procedures for international fare approval were streamlined, and gates at some of the busiest U.S. airports were dedicated to Canadian flights. The agreement extended both to passenger and all-cargo air services. The agreement with Mexico (1991) is not "open," but it liberalized trade to include open routes, no capacity restrictions, freedom to transfer cargo for "onward flights," and operational flexibility. The agreement restricted the number of airlines allowed to operate (one on any city pair segment) as well as double approval pricing.

As economic regulatory barriers fall, cabotage and other barriers remain (for example, technical regulations governing vehicle size and weights, driver certification and hours of service, and safety). As the rules on these matters diverge in the different countries (because of past national decisions on bridges, infrastructure, or social and political issues governing transport), the resulting inefficiencies in transborder areas will spur the demand for uniformity and harmonization.

Inconsistencies in transport regulations between countries that are part of a Free Trade Area will generate economic inefficiencies and disparate opportunities, thereby generating demand for harmonization. As production and transportation firms in all three countries rationalize their operations across the NAFTA region, transport nontariff barriers will cause inefficiencies and spur political demand for their relaxation. Because transportation carriers are required to operate around these restrictions, they have the direct effect of higher costs; the long-term indirect effect would be less competitive and efficient activities in the logistics industry and the consequent loss of productivity in the NAFTA region.

Rules of the Road:
The Complex Problem of Technical Regulation

In addition to economic regulation, transportation is subject to a host of technical regulations and standards. These include:

- Size and weight regulations for trucks
- Size, weight, and other technical standards for locomotives and other railroad stock
- Age, language, licensing, and health regulations for vehicle operators
- Conventions for road signs and traffic signals
- Procedures for ensuring vehicle safety
- Procedures governing transportation of hazardous goods.

In all of these cases, the three NAFTA partners have different regulations, standards, and procedures that have evolved over many years. Consequently, the cost of moving goods across borders is higher than the cost of moving the same goods the same distance domestically. This is one form of nontariff barrier.

Inconsistencies in truck size and weight regulations are a good example. These regulations are imposed for two reasons. The first is that excessively large vehicles will not operate effectively in mixed traffic streams, resulting in congestion, delays, and accidents. The second is that oversized vehicles result in accelerated wear and damage to road infrastructure and may result in the failure of bridges.

Truck size and weight regulations can be complex. For example, regulations may specify not only the gross weight of the truck, but also the weight per axle, the way the weight is distributed to the front and back axles, and the distance between the axles. Truck length regulations may

Table 2-4. Maximum Gross Vehicle Truck Weights in the NAFTA Countries
(kilograms)

Truck type	United States	Canada[a]	Mexico
Tractor–Semitrailer (5 axles)	36,288	39,500–41,500	44,000
Tractor–Semitrailer (6 axles)	36,288	46,500–53,000	48,500
Double trailer (6 axles)	36,288	47,600–43,500	47,500

a. Range of provincial regulations.

Source: North American Free Trade Agreement Land Transportation Standards Sub-committee, October 1997.

specify overall length, the length of tractor and trailer independently, or even the length of the trailer beyond the back-most axle.

Unfortunately, there are significant inconsistencies in these regulations in the three NAFTA partners. Even on the most basic dimension—gross truck weight—there is no consistency (table 2-4). The United States limits all trucks to a gross weight of 36,288 kilograms (80,000 pounds). Both Mexico and Canada allow higher weights for all categories of trucks, and they increase the weight limit for trucks with more than the standard five axles. This inconsistency is due mainly to conservative assumptions by U.S. officials about the maximum weight that can be supported by bridges.

To make matters worse, different regulations may apply in different places. For example, Canadian regulations are set at the provincial level, and despite recent efforts at standardization some variation remains across provinces. There are also some state-level variations in the United States, and different regulations apply on different parts of the highway network. (This is especially true for regulations applying to trucks hauling more than one trailer.)

These inconsistencies can add significantly to the cost of cross-border transportation. Indeed, some Canadian trucking firms must maintain separate fleets of trucks for shipments into the United States and for domestic shipments (Prentice and Wilson, 1998). Each country must ensure that trucks entering its territory are not in violation of its rules. This implies border inspections, which add to the cost of border operations and may contribute to costly border delays.

Recognizing the potential problems arising from inconsistencies in technical regulation of transportation, policymakers added a provision to NAFTA that established the Land Transportation Standards Subcommittee with responsibility for harmonization in all of the categories of technical regulation listed earlier. To date, significant progress has been made in the regulation of vehicle operators and in harmonization of road signs and signals. The issue of safety compliance, especially with reference to Mexican trucks coming into the United States, still presents problems, as we explain later in this chapter.

A special working group has concluded that complete harmonization is probably an unrealistic goal for a number of reasons. For one thing, carriers in all three countries have considerable investments in fleets designed for compliance with national regulations. Infrastructure design and construction in each country are based on assumptions that embody the national regulations. Finally, as with any question of harmonization, there is an important political dimension. Since international freight accounts for a relatively small percentage of trucking activity in the United States, the U.S. government is unlikely to change its regulations substantially. The other two partners, however, may see the adoption of U.S. rules as tantamount to sacrificing their political autonomy.

Borders as Barriers

Border crossing areas may be subject to long delays. This is partly because most national frontiers are crossed by a relatively small number of road and rail links, resulting in traffic bottlenecks. Furthermore, inspection and documentation activities that must occur as vehicles cross the border are time consuming. If delays at borders are long enough, they can add significantly to transport costs. Labor must be paid, and valuable vehicle capital must sit idle while waiting at the border crossing.

Canada and the United States have traded large volumes of goods for a number of decades, and in the process both governments have worked cooperatively to develop relatively efficient border-crossing routines. The border crossings along the U.S.-Mexican frontier are plagued by long delays, and many Mexican trucks must be sent back due to violations of various U.S. regulations.

Large volumes of freight movement at the U.S.-Mexican border are a more recent development, so there has been less time to work out the kinks. Illegal immigration and the transport of drugs in commercial vehicles also are major concerns. Finally, the Mexican truck fleet is in a relatively poor state, and Mexican carriers and drivers are not well informed on U.S regulations, so many trucks fail inspection.

The situation along the Mexican border has presented a major impediment to full implementation of NAFTA provisions. NAFTA specifies a timetable for providing full freedom of truck movement across the U.S.-Mexican border. Initially, Mexican trucks were allowed to operate only in a relatively small commercial zone extending a few miles into the territory of the four states that border Mexico. (Mexican goods bound for destinations outside this zone must be transferred to American trucks.) The NAFTA agreement set a deadline of December 1995 for Mexican trucks to be allowed to make deliveries throughout the territories of the border states and U.S. trucks to have similar access to Mexican border states. Mexico and the United States were to have an arrangement similar to the one that now exists between Canada and the United States. The 1995 deadline was delayed to 2000, but as of this writing, the access for Mexican trucks that was planned for 2000 had not yet been granted. The main reason for this delay is that the U.S. government and especially the governments of the bordering states fear that Mexican trucks will not meet U.S. regulations and may therefore cause accidents and damage infrastructure.

This would not be a problem if effective surveillance could be applied to prevent noncompliant trucks from entering the United States. The inspection process, however, must necessarily be highly complex because various federal agencies (Customs, Immigration and Naturalization, Department of Agriculture, Food and Drug Administration) all have concerns about what may cross the border in trucks. Inspection of the trucks themselves (as opposed to their contents or personnel) comes under the jurisdiction of state Departments of Transportation, which receive limited assistance from the U.S. Department of Transportation.

The checking by border states of trucks for size and weight violations and for safety violations (such as worn tires, improperly secured loads, inadequate brakes) is handicapped by the few inspectors assigned and by the micro infrastructural facilities available. With these limited facilities it is only possible to conduct spot inspections. As a result of these spot checks, roughly 50 percent of the trucks inspected have been put out of service due to some violation. Therefore, it is not surprising that state officials are reluctant to allow Mexican trucks to travel farther into their territories until either a more stringent inspection process can be put in place or a much lower rate of violation can be observed in spot checks.

There is considerable potential for new information and communication technologies that come under the general heading of Intelligent Transportation Systems (ITS). These systems can speed border crossings by eliminating much of the need for paper handling. They facilitate remote reading of truck identification and cargo information and basic checks on weight, length, height, and width while the truck is in motion. In addition, electronic databases can be used to identify trucks and drivers with previous violation histories so that inspection efforts can be concentrated on them.

Cooperative efforts are now under way to encourage the Mexican government to follow domestic inspection procedures that are more consistent with U.S. procedures. The objective of these efforts is to bring the general condition of the Mexican fleet up to a level where U.S. officials will permit it to have broader access to U.S. highways.

Conclusion and Lessons Learned

The high volume of trade in North America is not the result of a single free trade agreement. Rather, it has evolved over three decades due in large part to policies that have promoted the development of border-spanning industrial complexes, resulting in intra-industry trade of high value-added goods. In the case of Canada and the United States, this is the outcome of a sectoral trade agreement, the Auto Pact of 1965, while in the case of Mexico and the United States, it is the outcome of policies by both governments facilitating the development of the Maquiladora systems. Agricultural and resource commodities, which often figure prominently in public discussions of North American trade, make up a relatively small portion of the overall trade picture in the NAFTA area.

In light of this, it would be a mistake to imagine that the level of economic integration observed in North America will swiftly improve when tariff barriers are eliminated in some other part of the world. NAFTA is essentially a means of eliminating remaining trade barriers to create opportunities to expand and extend already well-established trade relations.

Despite the elimination of tariffs, truly "free" movement of goods across international frontiers is not a realty. Even if administrative nontariff barriers such as import licenses are removed and product standards are harmonized, a number of factors that are not normally associated with trade policy can create nontariff barriers that retard the cross-border flow of goods and prevent the full benefits of trade liberalization from being realized. In particular, factors that retard the integration of freight transportation systems within the free trade area and cause major delays in cross-border freight movements can serve as significant barriers to trade. In North America processes of transport deregulation and privatization have played complementary roles with trade liberalization to promote transport integration, but significant impediments to cross-border movement still remain. Areas of public policy that relate to border security (such as drugs and illegal immigration) also may pose major impediment to free movement across borders.

Among the specific lessons learned from the NAFTA experience are the following:

- Some of the greatest potential for trade within a free trade area lies in intra-industry trade in high value-added goods arising from cross-border integration of manufacturing industries. This type of integration may take decades to occur and may involve more than just the elimination of tariffs. It requires the development of an effective cross-border transit facilitation system.

- Inconsistencies in the economic regulation of transportation can impede the free movement of goods across borders. While in North America deregulation and privatization occurred in the years leading up to NAFTA, some residual regulations—especially in the form of cabotage rules or restrictions on the movement of certain goods—still increase the costs of cross-border shipment.
- Harmonization of technical standards, such as truck size and weight regulation, is a mundane issue that may not command much attention while the free trade treaty is being negotiated. The complexity of this issue, however, means that it may take a long time to sort out once the agreement has been made. This should at least be recognized when implementation timetables are drawn up.
- Agreement concerning technical standards is not enough. Methods of inspection and enforcement must ensure that each partner in the agreement adheres to the standards. Sufficient resources must be devoted to inspection activities at the border and elsewhere.
- The need to prevent undesired movements across borders—as in the case of drugs or illegal immigrants—can result in long delays that add significantly to the costs of international shipments, and therefore constitute one of the most important barriers to trade. Coordination between different government agencies to speed up border movements is critical.
- Factors that lead to delays at borders not only increase transportation costs, but also make it impossible to reap the productivity benefits associated with timely delivery services, as in the case of just-in-time inventories.

3

Transport Integration in the European Union

William P. Anderson

The European Union (EU) is the oldest and most highly evolved of the regional trading blocs that have developed in the second half of the twentieth century.[1] Comprising fifteen countries with combined populations of 375 million, it is of comparable size to the North American Free Trade Area (NAFTA). It has achieved, however, a much higher level of economic integration among its member states than has NAFTA. For one thing, there is much freer movement of labor across borders within the EU area than within the NAFTA area. Furthermore, EU member states must relinquish jurisdiction over a broader range of economic, social, and environmental policy areas.

Given the large number of national borders within the EU area, the integration of transportation markets and infrastructure and the harmonization of transportation policies are important preconditions for achieving free movement of goods and people. Establishment of a common transportation policy was a clearly stated goal in the founding documents. Little progress was made, however, on transportation policy during the first three decades of the European Union's existence. A number of factors account for this—most notably the presence of state-owned suppliers of transportation services and the desire by member governments to use transportation policy to promote their separate national economic programs.

The picture has changed considerably in the period after 1986, during which the European Union has launched programs to open up national markets in transportation services to competition from all member states

---

1. "European Union" is the most recent name for what was once called the "European Economic Community" and later called the "European Community."

and committed billions to projects that link up national infrastructure systems. This transition from inaction to activism is interesting not only for the types of policies that it entailed, but also for the roles played by the EU's powerful supranational institutions in bringing it about.

Historical Overview

The European Union is an institution that rose from the ashes of the Second World War. Its genesis had as much to do with promoting peace through interdependence as with reaping the gains from trade envisioned in economic theory. It evolved—as its early promoters had hoped it would—from a narrow sectoral and geographical jurisdiction to an economy-wide institution with members comprising most of the non-communist states of Europe.

Its precursor organization was the European Coal and Steel Community (ECSC), founded in 1951 to promote free movement of iron and steel as well as related raw materials such as coal and ore across borders. The impetus came from the French and German governments. They were joined by the Benelux countries (Belgium, the Netherlands, and Luxembourg), whose borders straddled critical iron and steel regions. The three nations had already established a custom union among themselves. Italy, which was anxious to build connections with the rest of Europe, also joined. (These countries came to be known as "the Six.") The goals of the ECSC were to promote efficiency in the basic industries and to thwart the formation of national cartels. It also wanted to prevent France and Germany from clashing over access to critical industrial resources, as they had in the years leading up to the war.

After a successful experiment with coal and steel, the governments of the Six embarked on a much broader integration project. The Treaty of Rome, which was signed in 1958, established the European Economic Community (EEC).[2] Under the treaty the Six agreed to a common external tariff and the phased elimination of all tariffs on goods traded within the EEC over a period of twelve years. But the treaty went beyond these traditional trade liberalization measures. It reduced barriers to free movement of people, capital, and services; reduced nontariff barriers such as inconsistent technical standards; established common policies in the areas of agriculture and transportation; and created two development institutions: the European Social Fund and the European Investment Bank (McCormick, 1999).

---

2. A second treaty, also signed by the Six in 1958, established the European Atomic Energy Community.

Achieving the program of the Treaty of Rome was a time-consuming and uneven process. Gradual progress was made on the harmonization of technical standards and the removal of restrictions on international labor movements, but neither of these tasks could be considered complete at the end of the 1990s. The Common Agricultural Policy did not come into force until 1968, and an effective Common Transport Policy came much later (see below).

Still, rapid growth in within-bloc trade and improvement in all development indicators attested to the success of the European Economic Community. During the 1970s and 1980s, other European countries saw the benefits of membership. After two vetoes by French governments under Charles de Gaulle, Britain's application for membership was finally accepted, and Britain, Ireland, and Denmark became full members in 1973. Three Southern European Countries—Portugal, Spain, and Greece—were added in the 1980s, bringing the membership to twelve. Finally Austria, Sweden, and Finland joined in the 1990s, bringing the total to fifteen. Future enlargement is likely, especially since many former members of the Soviet bloc (such as Poland, Hungary, and the Czech Republic) have shifted their economic orientations to the West. Turkey, with its huge market and rapidly industrializing economy, is also anxious to strengthen its European ties through membership.

Table 3-1 indicates that the enlargement of the EU area led to a more heterogeneous set of member states. The three new members from Southern Europe (Spain, Portugal, and Greece) have per capita incomes far below those of either the Six or new members from the North. There is also significant variation in the importance of trade in national economies. Total trade as a percentage of GDP is relatively low in Greece, Italy, Spain, and the United Kingdom when compared with Belgium, the Netherlands, and Ireland. All fifteen countries, however, trade at least 50 percent of both imports and exports within the Fifteen.

The Treaty on European Union, signed in Maastricht in 1992, marked a major step toward greater and more general integration of the member states. While the EEC had addressed certain elements of social policy, such as common rules on labor hours and conditions, its actions were generally limited to those meant to promote economic integration. Under the 1992 Treaty, jurisdiction was extended to areas less directly linked to the economy, such as consumer protection, public health, education, and (with Britain opting out) social policy. It also established the concept of European citizenship, allowing a national of any member state to live in any other member state, and set goals of achieving common policies for immigration and refugee status. On the economic front it set up the process for the most ambitious of all steps toward full integration: the establishment of a common currency. The 1992 Treaty is generally

Table 3-1. Demographic and Economic Characteristics of the EU Fifteen, by Country, 1998

Country	Population (millions)	Population growth (1990 = 100)	GDP (billions of ECUs)	GDP per capita (thousands of ECUs)	Exports (billions of ECUs)[a]	Percentage of exports to EU 15	Imports (billions of ECUs)[a]	Percentage of imports to EU 15	Total trade as a percentage of GDP
EU 15	374.6	103.8	7,472.5	19.9	1,976.2	63	1,896.4	62	52
Belgium	10.2	103.1	223.6	21.9	159.5	76	148.8	71	138
Denmark	5.3	102.9	150.9	28.5	43.8	67	41.9	70	57
Germany	82	105.4	1,910.3	23.3	482.5	56	413.4	58	47
Greece	10.5	105	107.8	10.3	9.5	52	25	66	32
Spain	39.3	101.8	507.7	12.9	93.3	71	111.6	68	40
France	58.7	105	1,274.5	21.7	286	62	274.5	68	44
Ireland	3.7	103	76	20.5	58.3	70	38.3	62	127
Italy	57.5	101.5	1,046.7	18.2	215.6	56	192.5	62	39
Luxembourg	0.4	113.2	15.5	38.8					
Netherlands	15.6	106.5	336.7	21.6	191.1	79	179.1	57	110
Austria	8.1	106.2	189.9	23.4	57.2	64	62	74	63
Portugal	9.9	99.3	95.7	9.7	21.6	82	32.9	77	57
Finland	5.1	104.2	115.5	22.6	39	56	29.4	66	59
Sweden	8.8	105.5	202.6	23	74.5	57	60.5	69	67
United Kingdom	59	103.5	1,220.4	20.7	244.3	58	286.5	53	43

a. Values for Belgium and Luxembourg are combined.
Source: European Commission (2000a, tables 1.3 and 1.4).

viewed as the date from which the "European Community" became the "European Union."

Institutions of the European Union

One factor that distinguishes the European Union from NAFTA is that the former is equipped with a set of powerful, supranational institutions that can make policy and even override the policies of member states. NAFTA has established independent review panels on domestic content rules and the environment, but they have narrow mandates, and most contentious issues must be addressed via intergovernmental negotiations.

The most conspicuous of the EU institutions is the European Commission, which is essentially the executive branch of the EU. There are twenty-two Directorates-General within the Commission with mandates for specific areas of administration such as external affairs, industry, environment, fisheries, and transport. These are assigned to a somewhat smaller group of Commissioners (some assume a portfolio of more than one Directorate). Commissioners are appointed by the member states, but they may not be members of the current government and must swear in their oath of office to put EU interests ahead of national interest. The Commission has a president who is appointed for a five-year term, renewable once.

In addition to its administrative responsibilities, the Commission initiates all EU legislation. Bills are passed from the Commission to the European Parliament for approval and amendment. Since it does not have the power to initiate legislation, the Parliament is a relatively weak body. It is, however, of symbolic importance as the only directly elected legislature of any supranational institution, and its powers have increased gradually, especially as a result of the 1992 Treaty.

Final approval of legislation is by the Council of Ministers, which is made up of representatives of the member state governments. The composition of this council actually depends upon the proposal under consideration. For example, legislation relating to the Common Transport Policy would be approved by the transport ministers of the fifteen states, while legislation relating to the Common Agricultural Policy would be approved by the agriculture ministers. The Council of Europe, comprising the heads of government (prime minister or president) from each member state, takes up very high level issues.

The EU also has its own judicial institution, the European Court of Justice. The ECJ has the critical responsibility of ruling on whether the laws and actions of national governments are consistent with EU law and whether laws implemented by the EU according to the legislative process described above are consistent with the Treaty of Rome and all later EU treaties. History has shown that the European Court of Justice plays a critical role in bringing the goals expressed in the treaties to fruition. This is especially true in the case of transport policy, which is discussed below.

While these supranational institutions give the EU a degree of authority that is greater than that of other trade blocs, its power is limited by the *principle of subsidiarity,* which prevents the EU from interfering in policy decisions that can be taken effectively at the national level. As already stated, however, the range of policy areas where joint decisionmaking is considered more effective has expanded steadily throughout the history of the EU.

Transportation in the European Union

The goal of establishing a common transportation policy was stated explicitly in the Treaty of Rome. For almost thirty years, however, many observers viewed harmonization of transportation systems within the EU as a conspicuous failure (Button, 1993; McCormick, 1999; European Commission, 1999). Before reviewing the reasons for this situation and the corrective actions that have been taken in recent years, we offer some background on transportation within the EU Fifteen.

Commercial transportation services account for approximately 4 percent of the combined GDP of the EU Fifteen. This rises to 7 percent if own-account operations and private transportation are included, making transportation larger than either the agriculture or steel sectors (European Commission, 1999). But this understates the general importance of transportation in the EU economy, as high-quality freight and passenger service between member states play critical roles in realizing the economic benefits of increased economic integration.

Figures 3-1, 3-2, and 3-3 provide a statistical overview of the level and modal distribution of transportation activity related to movements within the EU. (Figures 3-1 and 3-2 include U.S. domestic transportation data for the purpose of comparison.) Figure 3-1 indicates that despite the fact that the population of the European Union is greater than that of the United States, the level of internal personal transportation (measured in passenger kilometers) is higher in the United States. This reflects in part the more compact settlement pattern in the EU and is probably also attributable in some measure to lower rates of car ownership and other factors affecting personal mobility. While passenger car travel is dominant in both, rail and public transit have larger shares in the European Union, while air travel is more important in the United States.

Unlike in personal transportation, rail plays a smaller role in EU freight transportation than it does in U.S. freight transportation (figure 3-2). On

Figure 3-1. Passenger Transport within the European Union and the United States, 1997

Billions of passenger kilometers

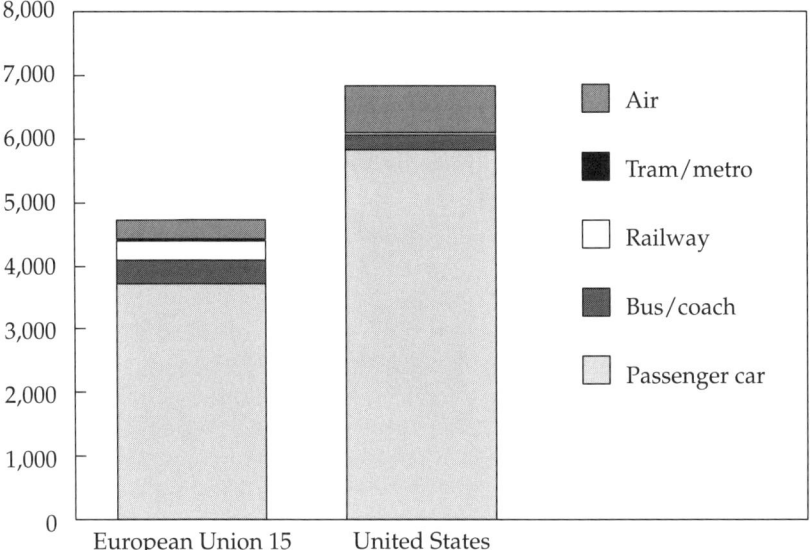

Source: European Commission (2000a, table 9.4).

the other hand, a much higher proportion of EU goods is shipped by sea. (Note that sea transportation here refers only to domestic and inter-EU shipments.) The evolution of this modal breakdown for freight is illustrated in figure 3-3. Total ton kilometers roughly doubled between 1970 and 1997, with nearly all the growth occurring in two modes: road and sea.

The decline of rail in both relative and absolute terms reflects a large measure of substitution of road transportation for rail. It may also be the case that the relatively poor level of interoperability among national railways has prevented rail from capturing a significant share of the rapidly growing intercountry trade. One likely explanation for the growth of sea transportation is the addition of the United Kingdom, Ireland, Sweden, and Finland, all of which trade with the rest of Europe primarily by sea. The addition of Portugal, Spain, and Greece probably contributed to this trend because of the limits on land transportation across the Pyrenees and Balkans.

Figure 3-2. Freight Transport within the European Union and the United States, 1997

Billions of total metric ton kilometers

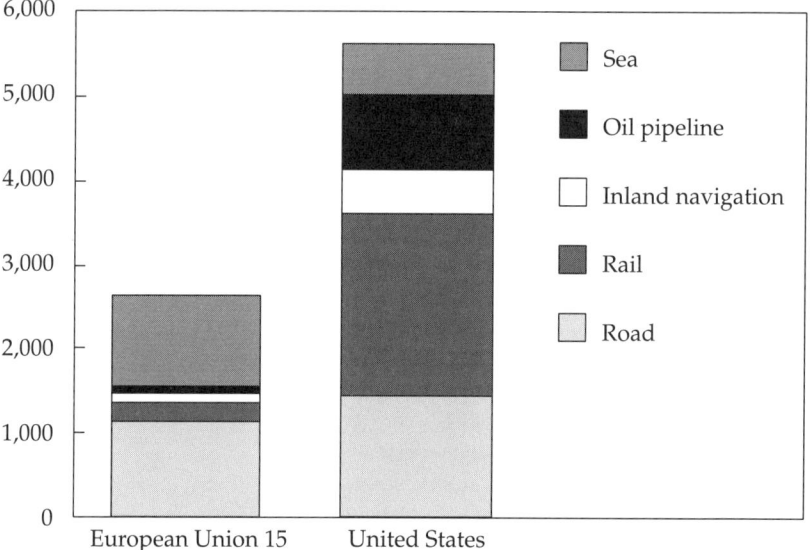

Source: European Commission (2000a, table 9.4).

Creating an integrated transportation system within the EU area requires progress on three interrelated objectives: interoperability, free market access, and interconnection. Interoperability refers to the harmonization of technical standards for infrastructure elements ranging from rail gauge to air traffic control systems as well as rules applying to service providers such as truck size and weight restrictions. Free market access refers to the removal of restrictions that prevent providers of transportation services based in one member state from operating in another. Interconnection refers to the problem of linking up national infrastructure networks. Connections among these networks were relatively sparse because many borders coincide with physical barriers such as mountains, rivers, and seas. The lack of connections also reflects the fact that national networks have been developed primarily to meet the domestic needs of member states.

The reasons for slow progress in achieving these goals are varied, but most relate to the traditional mandate of national governments in trans-

Figure 3-3. Goods Transport within the European Union, 1970–97

Billions of total metric ton kilometers

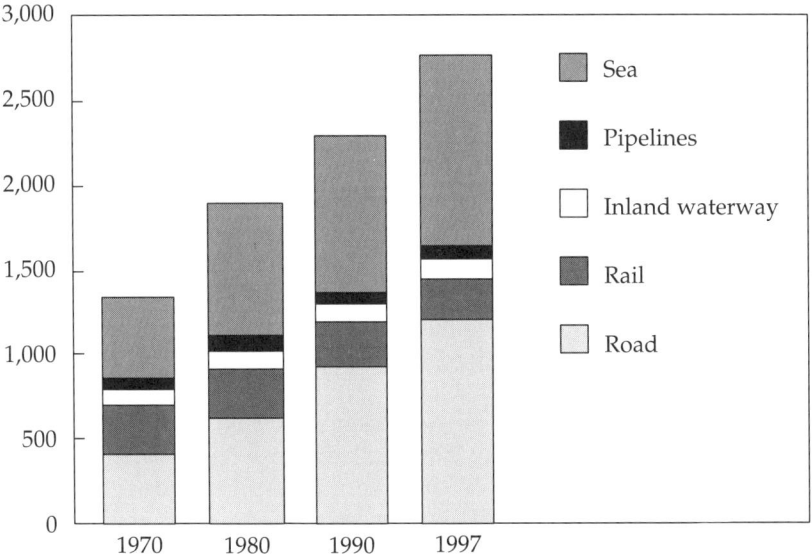

Source: European Commission (2000a, table 4.2).

portation policy and their unwillingness to transfer authority to the EU. For example, nearly all national governments were owners of major transportation suppliers, including railways and airlines, and therefore they had interests in preserving their local monopoly powers. Furthermore, transportation policy is frequently used as a means of pursuing national economic goals. The role of subnational and even local governments in transportation complicates the process of harmonization further. Thus, the member states had some interest in preserving the status quo of policy fragmentation.

By the 1980s, groups representing consumers of transportation services who were increasingly frustrated with high costs and poor quality began to bring both political and judicial pressure on the European Union to take action. In 1985 the European Court of Justice had ruled that the European Commission had failed to act appropriately to implement the Common Transport Policy required under the Treaty of Rome. This ruling related specifically to opening up national transportation markets to suppliers from other member states, but it marked a major turning point after which the Commission and Parliament became more active in all aspects of transportation policy.

Between 1987 and 1992 major new legislation was enacted regarding air, marine, road, rail, and inland water transportation. This legislation dealt mostly with issues of market access and interoperability, as well as common work rules for transportation employees. In the 1990s, however, the Commission began to focus more on issues of interconnection. For example, a 1993 White Paper on growth, competitiveness, and employment emphasized the transformations in production systems, methods of organizing work, and consumption patterns that were already being adopted in North America and Asia. Economic fragmentation and adherence to traditional practices made it difficult for European businesses to manage complex value chains and spawn small innovative firms, placing the EU in a weak competitive position vis-à-vis other major production regions.

Repeating a goal that had already been enshrined in the 1992 Treaty on European Union, the White Paper called for the development of integrated and complementary information, transportation, and energy Trans-European Networks (TENs). This led to the announcement in 1994 of a major infrastructure program specifically geared to filling gaps in the existing European transportation networks.

Interoperability

Achieving interoperability in transportation systems involves two related tasks. The first is to see that all new infrastructures incorporate a common set of design standards. The second is to ensure that equipment and employees operating on existing infrastructure meet a common set of technology and safety standards. The program for achieving interoperability in high-speed train (HST) networks is an example of the first task.

Because most ongoing HST projects receive some support under the TEN program (see below), the European Union is well placed to ensure consistency of technical standards. However, under the "new approach" to interoperability, the goal is to establish only those common standards that are necessary to achieve a smooth interface between systems, rather than stifle innovation by insisting on a full set of common specifications. A body known as the European Association for Inter-operability is charged with proposing an appropriate set of Technical Specifications for Interoperability (TSI). This body is made up of representatives from railways and related industries, rather than officials from either the Commission or member state governments. The TSI are submitted to the

Commission, which approves them after consultation with an expert committee (European Commission, 1999, Doc. 1.1.2).

Adopting and enforcing a common set of road vehicle weight and dimension standards are preconditions for interoperability. A new set of standards was adopted in 1996 to apply to vehicles operating throughout the EU. These include the maximum length, height, and weight for different categories of trucks, including "road trains" that can be as long as 18.75 meters and weigh up to 44 metric tons (European Commission, 1999, Doc. 2.13.1).

Given the complex nature of these regulations, checks at borders to ensure that incoming trucks meet regulations can be time consuming. Given the high level of harmonization of EU standards, however, it has been determined that such checks are no longer necessary. Since all EU trucks must conform to common standards, there is no reason to treat domestic and foreign trucks any differently. Thus foreign trucks can be subjected to the same spot-checking procedures that are used for domestic trucks, and authorizations for cabotage can be checked at the same time. Border checks for control of both authorization and size and weight rules were eliminated at the end of 1989 (European Commission, 1999, Doc. 2.11.1).

Market Access

Rules of market access for transportation services have been contentious since the inception of the EU. The final language of the Treaty of Rome left considerable room for interpretation. For example, while the Treaty committed the member states to a Common Transport Policy, it did not call for a common market in transportation. Also, specific reference was made only to road, rail, and inland waterways, leaving the impression that air and sea transport were excluded from EU control. Furthermore, competition (antitrust) rules contained language excluding transportation.

Air transportation is an especially interesting case. Until the 1980s, all member states had ownership interests in national flagship airlines. These airlines had long been considered instruments of national economic policy, and influential public sector unions dominated their labor forces. Furthermore, national airlines were a matter of prestige for most states. Member states were loath to allow competition that might threaten the viability of national flagship carriers, despite the fact that most of them lost money.

Regulation on intercountry service was handled via bilateral arrangements whereby the two national governments designated carriers, defined timetables, set fares, and divided the revenues (O'Reilly and Sweet,

1998). For the most part, independent carriers were closed out of these routes. Foreign carriers were given access only to major national airports, with service to regional airports limited to national carriers.

Impetus for change came primarily from business groups, which argued that the poor quality and high cost of air travel within the European Union was a major barrier to economic integration and global competitiveness. They had a sympathetic ear in the European Commission: its 1979 attempt to institute a program of airline liberalization had been thwarted by the member states. By the middle of the 1980s, business groups also had the support of two member governments—the United Kingdom and the Netherlands—that had begun their own deregulation initiatives.

An example of the objections of member states is provided by Greece, which argued that economic, regional development, and security priorities depended upon year-round service between the mainland and the Greek islands. If independent operators were allowed into this market, they would offer services only during the lucrative summer tourist season, leaving the unprofitable months to the national carrier.

A key event in the breakdown of the old system came when the French government prosecuted some independent airlines offering domestic services below the regulated fares. A French court referred the case to the European Court of Justice, which found that although air travel was protected from some elements of competition policy, it was not completely immune and that the European Commission had some authority regarding airline practices.

In the aftermath of this decision, the Commission attempted for the second time to reform air travel. It did not propose a wholesale American-style deregulation, but rather that national regulation regarding intercountry flights be removed in favor of a EU regulatory regime. Under a new set of rules agreed upon in 1987, many of the old restrictions remained, but avenues for greater competition were created including:

- permission for carriers to offer restricted service with fares discounted below the reference rate approved by the two member states;
- a requirement that each state permit more than one airline from another state access to its airports (although not necessarily more than one to the same airport);
- under some restrictions, permission for carriers to offer service to a regional airport in another country; and
- under carefully controlled circumstances, permission for an airline from one country to provide service between two other countries.

Note that an airline in one country still cannot offer service between two points within another country or cabotage (O'Reilly and Sweet, 1998).

The result of this transformation is a more competitive and efficient environment but not a fully deregulated one. This environment led to a restructuring of the industry, including the emergence of cut-rate carriers and a number of international alliances. The benefits have been greater choice and lower fares for EU air travelers (McCormick, 1999).

In those areas of transportation services where governments have been less involved in the supply side, much greater strides have been made toward achieving a true common market. Transportation of freight by road (trucking) is a good example. Under 1992 regulations, any operator with a "community authorization" has unlimited access to the market for freight movement between member states. This includes trips beginning or ending in the state where the carrier is based and trips between any other two states.

The liberal community market access rules also extend to cabotage. Starting in 1990, any carrier with a "community cabotage authorization" can carry goods within any state in the EU Fifteen. These authorizations were issued under an increasing quota system until 1998, when all quotas were removed (European Commission 2000b). Complementary rules with respect to licensing of and work rules for drivers and other employees are also in place.

There are provisions to protect national trucking industries from extreme damage from foreign competitors with either community or community cabotage authorization. If a significant number of domestic firms are found to be in danger of severe financial damage, a crisis period is declared during which market access is restricted. The restrictions are imposed for six months, renewable once (European Commission, 1999).

Developing Trans-European Networks

As part of its Trans-European Networks (TEN) initiative, the EU embarked in the 1990s on a program to encourage transportation infrastructure projects that fill the gaps in existing Europe-wide networks. The total cost of filling the gaps in transportation and energy networks was estimated to be in excess of 400 billion ECUs over fifteen years, only a small proportion of which could be provided from EU funds. A program assessed proposed projects on the basis of their contribution to the objectives of the TEN initiative and selected a limited number to which EU support would be provided up to a limit of 10 percent of total project costs. This is in contrast to earlier practice when limited funds were distributed at the discretion of the Directorate General for Transport across many infrastructure projects proposed by member states (Kinnock, 1995). Under the new program the funds are in the form of co-financing for feasibility studies, fees for loan guarantees, interest rate subsidies, and (in limited circumstances) direct investment grants. The remaining 90 percent of funds must come from member states and the private sector under public-private partnership arrangements (Kinnock, 1995).

In 1994, fourteen priority projects, with total combined project costs of 90 billion ECUs, were designated for EU support (up to a maximum of 9 billion.) They are listed in table 3-2. Six are high-speed rail projects, only one is for airport facilities, and the rest are for conventional rail, road, and multimodal projects. Each of these project can be viewed in terms of its contribution to creating a truly trans-European transportation system. For example, Project 1 adds two new North-South segments to an existing high-speed corridor between Nuremberg and Munich so that an integrated rail corridor for both freight and passengers is available from Northeast Germany to the economic heartland of Italy. This is complementary to Project 6, a high-speed corridor from southern France to the Adriatic.

Project 13 attempts to bring Ireland closer to the mainland of Europe by means of a land-sea link across Great Britain. The objective is to provide high-quality road/ferry service linking the three largest cities in Ireland (Cork, Dublin, and Belfast) to the East Coast English Ports with well-established ferry services to ports in Belgium and the Netherlands.

In a similar way Project 11 seeks to link the northern periphery of the EU with mainland Europe, but in this case by means of a bridge/tunnel project for both rail and highway connection between Sweden and Denmark. The benefits of this link will be extended throughout Scandinavia by means of Project 12, which establishes multimodal corridors linking the main centers of Sweden and Finland and providing superior access to the non-EU states of Norway and the Russian Federation.

Conclusions

The experience of the European Union as it tries to develop an integrated transport system provides some valuable lessons for other trading blocs. The EU has achieved some things—such as elimination of border checks and full cabotage in some service categories—that NAFTA may not achieve for decades. Still, the process has been painful and remains very incomplete after almost fifty years.

One important lesson is that member states have strong incentives to cling to the status quo of fragmented transportation infrastructure and regulation. Ownership of major supply entities is one reason. Privatization in groups such as the Common Market of the South (*Mercado Comin del Sur*, or Mercosur) should make the process of transportation integration simpler. Also, transportation policy is an instrument for pursuing national economic goals that member governments will not relinquish easily.

Table 3-2. Trans-European Networks: Fourteen Priority Transportation Projects

Project and route
1. High speed train/combined transport North-South (Berlin-Verona)
2. High speed train (Paris-Brussels-Cologne-Amsterdam-London)
3. High speed train South (Madrid-Barcelona-Montpellier/Madrid-Vitoria-Dax)
4. High speed train (Paris-eastern France-southern Germany; includes Metz-Luxembourg branch)
5. Conventional rail/Betuwe Line combined transport (Rotterdam-German border)
6. High speed train/combined transport France-Italy (Lyon-Turin-Milan-Venice-Trieste)
7. Greek motorways: PATHE (North-South axis: Rio-Antirio to Bulgarian border) and via Egnatia (East-West axis, Igoumenitsa to Turkish border)
8. Multimodal link (integrated road, rail, maritime, and air facilities) between Iberian Peninsula and Central Europe
9. Conventional rail link (Cork-Dublin-Belfast-Larne-Stanraer)
10. Air hub for northern Italy (Malpensa Airport) with intermodal facilities for road and rail
11. Fixed rail/road link between Copenhagen, Denmark, and Malmö, Sweden–Oresund fixed link (bridge-tunnel)
12. Nordic triangle: integrated road and rail system connecting major cities in Denmark, Sweden, and Finland, with sea link between Sweden and Finland
13. Ireland–United Kingdom–Benelux road and ferry service link
14. High speed train/combined transport West Coast Main Line (United Kingdom)

Source: European Commission (1998).

The second, and related, lesson is that achieving major integration goals may require strong, supranational institutions. The European Court of Justice has played a critical role in breaking down traditional national prerogatives that stood in the way of a Common Transport Policy for thirty years. In the case of air transportation, the European Commission put forth an argument for regulatory reform that was opposed by all member states in 1979 but after almost a decade of debate and litigation came into force.

4

Transport and Trade in Mercosur

T. R. Lakshmanan

The contemporary development landscape is undergoing radical changes in the context of technological advances in communications, transportation, and production, and in a global economy where services, information, and knowledge are an increasing portion of economic value. Multinational companies depend on production chains that span several countries. Materials and components from different countries are assembled in yet another country, with distribution and marketing in other locales in response to worldwide consumer signals. This slicing of the "value chain" leads to an increasingly competitive global economic environment. A rising number of countries can offer high-quality, low-cost production as well as speedy, time-definite delivery of goods at competitive prices.

In response, many countries have clustered together in regional trading blocs and strive to create dynamic comparative advantages to facilitate their insertion in the global economy on favorable terms. The European Community (EC) and the North American Free Trade Agreement (NAFTA) signatories (the United States, Canada, and Mexico) illustrate this development. In keeping with this trend, four countries in South America—Argentina, Brazil, Paraguay, and Uruguay—signed the Treaty of Asuncion on March 26, 1991, to create on January 1, 1995, the Common Market of the South (*Mercado Comin del Sur* or Mercosur). Chile and Bolivia joined as associate members in 1996; they participate in the Free Trade Area (FTA) but not the common external tariff (CET) or the planned Common Market.

Mercosur has several antecedents in Latin America. The first is the Latin American Free Trade Association (LAFTA), created in 1960 to eliminate trade barriers and also to foster the then-prevalent import substitution strategy (IS) of industrialization through the provision of economies

51

of scale with the larger markets of the FTA. However, this multilateral agreement did not take root since the IS strategy, while achieving a significant level of industrialization, led to highly protected national markets: the tariff levels ranged in this era from 41 percent in Brazil to 110 percent in Argentina (Coffey, 1998). LAFTA and its successor (the Latin American Integration Association or ALADI), which tried to liberalize trade and coordinate macroeconomic policies, were consequently delayed and postponed, as the import substitution model collapsed in Latin America in the 1980s.

In the 1980s and 1990s, however, economic and political developments converged to speed up the creation of Mercosur. First, in the emerging global economy and cross-country production networks, trade liberalization offers great benefits for Latin American countries: new export markets, international technology transfers, increasing efficiency through heightened competition, and integration into the global production networks noted above, which account for a third of all world trade (World Bank, 1999). Integration into global production value-chain networks is feasible if the Latin American countries liberalize and improve their transportation and communication systems so that they offer fast and reliable delivery of goods and coordination across borders. In the absence of worldwide liberalization, regional trade agreements are second-best solutions (if they lead to drops in consumer and producer prices).

Second, the creation of Mercosur was prompted by developing countries' growing perception that the Uruguay Round Agreement, which incorporated agriculture into multilateral trade negotiations, was not very helpful to them. It did not offer much market access for Latin American countries that export agricultural commodities without subsidies (OECD, 1998).

Third, the deep economic crisis in the Southern Cone countries and their increasingly marginal role in world trade took on the character of security issues in the late 1980s. The consequent drive to be a more active participant in world trade provided another stimulus to the creation of Mercosur.

Finally, in some countries there were supportive political changes (such as democratization processes, security and peace concerns in the Southern Cone, and a changing perception of the state's role in the economy) that promoted deregulation and liberalization of trade regimes. These changes set in motion in Argentina and Brazil a variety of presidential-level initiatives in economic integration, foreign policy, and security cooperation. As large trading blocs emerged in North America, Europe, and East Asia, Latin American decisionmakers' desire not to be cut off from the ongoing reconfiguration of the global economy strengthened incentives to seek and pursue closer economic links among themselves (Manzetti, 1994).

Treaty of Asuncion

The creation of Mercosur by the Treaty of Asuncion in 1991 thus represents a confluence of powerful economic and political developments on the global and regional levels (Manzetti, 1994; Roett, 1999; Hirst, 1999). As a consequence, in contrast to the experience of other Free Trade Areas such as NAFTA, where economic integration was achieved gradually through a series of stages (Lakshmanan and Anderson, 1999), Mercosur countries bypassed several intermediate steps when they initiated a common market in 1995 and planned for a Customs Union by 2006. A Common Market among the participating members is foreseen eventually.

The key objective of the Treaty of Asuncion is the integration of Mercosur economies and an increase in the competitiveness of the integrated economies by facilitating the free flow of goods, services, and factors of production among the member countries. The treaty also was intended to promote a variety of supporting policies, including privatization, deregulation, reduction of the public sector's role in the economy in order to attract foreign direct investment, and coordination of member countries' macroeconomic policies to ensure economic stability and adequate competitive situations. The specific provisions of the treaty cover four main areas: tariff elimination, a common external tariff, coordination of macroeconomic policies, and an institutional structure for dispute resolution.

Tariff Elimination

Tariffs were reduced according to schedule in order to attain a zero tariff for Argentina and Brazil by January 1995 and for Uruguay and Paraguay by January 1996. Furthermore, import quotas and nonquantitative restrictions were to be phased out under the Treaty of Asuncion. Chile's agreement to become an associate member allows it to retain its external tariff of 11 percent on virtually all imports from nonmembers of Mercosur. A significant aspect of the Chile agreement is the physical integration protocol, which allows for the development of cross-border projects, mostly mining and infrastructure, that can be undertaken immediately without extended negotiations between the governments of the affected countries

Common External Tariff

The creation of a Customs Union required the establishment of a common external tariff in goods. As Coffey (1998) notes, CET will become applicable for capital goods by 2001 and for telecommunications and information by 2006. Some sectors, such as autos, textiles, and sugar, will remain subject to national rules until a common regime can be agreed upon. Government procurement and some sensitive industries are still not part of a common trade policy.

Although advances have occurred in CET development and implementation, complex issues arise because of differences in the industrial mixes of the member countries. The Mercosur region is a net exporter of most agricultural products at internationally competitive prices. Therefore, CET for these commodities was set by Mercosur at relatively low levels—in part to neutralize the highly subsidized agricultural exports from North America and Europe (OECD, 1998).

Differences in the composition of manufacturing in the member countries raised tough issues. Argentina does not have significant industries in capital goods, computers, or consumer goods, and it levies zero tariffs on these goods; Brazil, the only producer of computers and the largest producer of capital goods, would like protection for a period during which structural adjustment could provide Brazilian producers the ability to compete at zero tariff. A period of transition was agreed upon—an average tariff of 14 percent for capital goods until 2001, and a 16 percent tariff for computers and some telecommunications goods until 2006.

There are also national lists of exceptions to CET. The exceptions list for Brazil is weighted in the chemical and petrochemical sectors, milk products, and raw materials for the textiles industry; in Argentina, the weighting is in the steel and chemical, paper, and footwear sectors; in Paraguay and Uruguay, the exceptions are in the agricultural sectors (Mye and Palagonia, 1996). Common external tariffs covered 87 percent of the tariff items in 1997, and Mercosur is expected to be a true Customs Union by 2006 (Pereira, 1999).

Coordination of Macroeconomic Policies

Members of Mercosur agreed to cooperate through coordination of their economic policies, such as fiscal and monetary policies, foreign exchange, and capital movements. In addition, they strive to harmonize sectoral policies in agriculture, manufacturing, services, transport and communications, and customs.

Institutional Structure for Dispute Resolution

The institutional structure for dispute resolution is not yet well articulated. It includes the highest ranking body, the Common Market Council, comprising member countries' foreign and economic ministers; the implementing organ, GMC (Grupo Mercado Comun); an effective system of panels for dispute settlements; and a technical body for the analysis and resolution of pending disputes within Mercosur and with third parties.

Mercosur Partners and Their Evolving Integration

Mercosur is the largest trading bloc comprised entirely of developing countries. Figure 4-1 compares its market size and that of NAFTA, the European Union, and several large countries. In 1998 Mercosur represented a $1.2 trillion economy with 233 million inhabitants and a per capita income of US$6,932.

Mercosur member countries are a diverse lot in terms of physical size, demographic levels and composition, level of income, industrial composition, and the role of trade in their economies. Brazil and Argentina dominate this bloc, accounting for 82 percent of the physical area, 83.6 percent of the population, and 90.8 percent of the GNP. Chile, Argen-

Figure 4-1. GNP of Mercosur and of Other Selected Markets, 1998

Billions of U.S. dollars

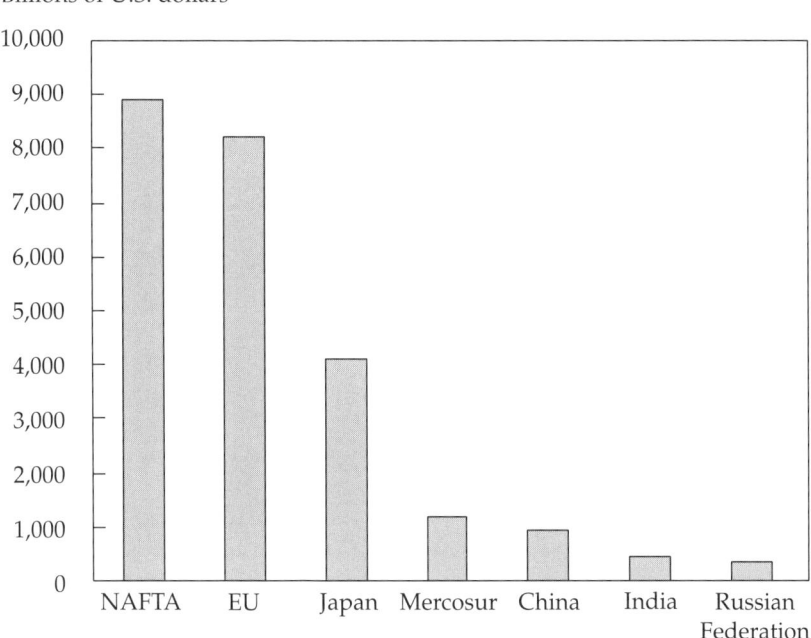

Source: World Bank (2000b).

tina, and Uruguay are more urbanized and have the higher per capita incomes. International trade is more important in the smaller countries, ranging from 43 percent of the GNP in Bolivia and Uruguay to 60 percent in Chile and 100 percent in Paraguay.

Tables 4-1and 4-2 show the progress of selected economic indicators in the 1990s. The 1990–98 period was one of demographic expansion and considerable growth of incomes and trade. It is worth noting that trade is not a large portion of GNP in Argentina and Brazil.

The trade performance of Mercosur since the signing of the Treaty of Asuncion in 1991 is impressive, indicating a significant and growing interdependence among the member economies. While trade with non-member countries increased between 1991 and 1997 (from US$69.3 billion to US$138.2 billion), expanding at 12 percent and above the world average, trade within Mercosur quadrupled during the same period (from US$10.3 billion to US$41.3 billion), as derived from table 4-3. In this part of the world intraregional trade has been a low portion of total trade because the member countries' semicolonial trade links to European and North American economies historically have been stronger than their trade links with one another. Yet intramember trade (as a percentage of total trade) has risen. In 1997 it accounted for 24.9 percent of exports and 21.4 percent of imports. The largest expansion occurred between Brazil and Argentina. Argentina is now the second trading partner of Brazil after the United States. After a quarter century of unsatisfactory efforts at trade integration, this explosive growth in intraregional trade augers well for Mercosur. The recent growth rates of intraregional exports in Mercosur are higher than those of other Western Hemisphere regions' exports and reflect well on Mercosur's trade integration prospects (table 4-4).

The composition of intramember trade is weighted heavily (more than in extraregional exports) toward industrial products that exhibit moderate to high technological intensity (table 4-5). In 1996, commodities and semiprocessed goods accounted for 43 percent, and manufactured goods for 56 percent, of total intramember exports (Markwald and Machado, 1999). If one examines the technological intensity of exports, intra-Mercosur exports have a higher proportion of the middle levels of technical intensity than exports to the European Union or to Asia, which seem to draw mostly low technology goods. NAFTA occupies an intermediate position, with a higher share of manufactured goods, especially labor-intensive goods, as well as aircraft purchases from Brazil.

This combination of rapid quantitative growth of intraregional trade and a trade composition rich in capital-intensive goods is ground for an optimistic assessment of Mercosur's performance. In the larger context of developing economies, the promising evolution in trade is a particu-

Table 4-1. Selected Economic Indicators of Mercosur, by Year, 1990–95

Indicator	1990	1991	1992	1993	1994	1995
Per capita income (U.S. dollars)	2,943	3,105	3,201	3,435	3,889	4,764
Exports (billions of U.S. dollars)	46.8	46.3	50.7	54.7	63.0	71.4
Imports (billions of U.S. dollars)	27.3	31.8	38.0	45.2	58.6	74.5
Trade balance (billions of U.S. dollars)	19.5	14.5	12.7	9.5	4.4	–3.1
Current account (billions of U.S. dollars)	0.76	–2.5	–1.6	–9.2	–12.6	–21.5
International reserves (billions of U.S. dollars)	13.8	16.4	34.4	46.5	53.9	66.7
Trade as a percentage of GNP	13.0	13.0	13.0	13.0	15.7	15.0

Source: OECD (1998).

Table 4-2. Demographic and Economic Characteristics of Mercosur, by Country, 1996–98

Indicator	Argentina	Brazil	Paraguay	Uruguay	Chile	Bolivia	Total
Area (millions of square kilometers)	2.8	8.5	0.4	0.2	0.8	1.1	13.8
Population (millions)							
1996	34.7	164.0	5.0	3.2	14.5	7.6	229.0
1998	36.0	166.0	5.2	3.3	14.8	7.9	233.2
GNP[a]							
1996	282.2	701.5	9.0	17.8	59.1	6.9	1,076.5
1998	324.1	758.0	9.2	20.3	71.3	7.9	1,190.8
GNP per capita[b]							
1998	10,200	6,160	3,650	9,480	12,890	2,820	6,932
Percentage of the population in urban areas, 1998	89	80	55	91	84	63	
Growth rates, 1990–98 (percent)							
GNP	5.3	3.3	2.8	3.9	7.9	4.2	
Gross domestic investment	12.5	3.9	3.6	8.3	13.9	6.9	
Exports of goods and services	9.3	5.6	7.3	8.0	9.8	6.7	
Exports[a]							
1996	23.8	47.7	2.7	2.4	15.3	1.1	93.0
1998	29.4	60.3	4.3	4.3	20.6	1.4	120.3
Imports[a]							
1996	22.1	47.7	2.7	2.4	15.3	1.1	93.0
1998	35.0	79.8	5.0	4.5	22.2	2.0	148.5
Trade as percentage of GNP 1998	19.8	18.5	100	43.3	60	43	
Foreign direct investment[a] 1997	6.6	19.7	0.3	0.2	5.4	0.6	32.8

a. Billions of U.S. dollars.
b. U.S. dollars at purchasing power parity.
Source: World Bank (2000b, 230–71).

Table 4-3. Intraregional Trade in Mercosur, 1991–97

Trade	1991	1997	Growth per year, 1991–97 (%)
Exports			
Total (billions of U.S. dollars)	45.9	82.9	10.4
Within Mercosur (percent)	11.1	24.9	26.3
Outside Mercosur (percent)	88.9	75.1	7.3
Imports			
Total (billions of U.S. dollars)	34.3	96.7	18.9
Within Mercosur (percent)	15.3	21.4	25.7
Outside Mercosur (percent)	84.7	78.6	17.4

Source: The data were adapted from Markwald and Machado (1999, 63).

larly gratifying experience for a mid-size trading bloc comprised entirely of developing economies.

Does this suggest that the integration project—established to exploit the economies of scale and gains from specialization (as well as to use the larger regional market as a platform from which Mercosur could be inserted competitively into the global economy)—is progressing toward those goals? One study comes to a contrary inference, suggesting that there has been trade diversion, since the dynamic products of Mercosur intratrade are in capital-intensive sectors in which member countries have not had strong export performance (Yeats, 1997). Critics of the Yeats study take the view that it would have been more accurate (in determining the balance between creation and diversion of trade) to look at members' imports (Markwald and Machado, 1999).

Table 4-4. Western Hemisphere Exports, 1996 and 1997

(percentage change)

Region	Destination	1996	1997
Mercosur	Within Mercosur	18.4	21.4
	Outside Mercosur	3.5	7.9
NAFTA	Within NAFTA	10.6	10.7
	Outside NAFTA	4.6	6.7
Latin America	Within Latin America	4.5	21.6
	Outside Latin America	11.3	9.3

Source: Safadi and Yeats (1993).

Table 4-5. Exports of Industrialized Goods from Argentina and Brazil, by Level of Technological Intensity, 1992–96
(percent)

Level of technological intensity	Inside Mercosur, 1996	Outside Mercosur, 1996			Annual growth, 1992–96	
		NAFTA	EU	Asia	Inside Mercosur[a]	Outside Mercosur[b]
Low	31.4	54.7	74.2	71.8	22.2	8.2
Low-average	26.0	19.1	12.9	17.8	21.2	2.3
Average-high	39.6	16.1	10.0	10.3	21.8	2.5
High	3.0	10.1	2.9	0.7	27.5	5.6

a. 21.9 percent for all industrial goods.
b. 6.2 percent for all industrial goods.
Source: Markwald and Machado (1999, 6).

Table 4-6. Intra-industry Trade, 1992

(percent)

Country	Brazil	Argentina	United States	European Union
Brazil	—	73.0	64.0	55.0
Argentina	56.0	—	30.0	23.0

Source: OECD (1998, 24).

While the potential dynamic advantages of integration have not yet been realized in the few years Mercosur has been in operation, intra-industrial linkages within manufacturing sectors have already improved. Since intra-industrial trade is a major source of dynamism in global trade and in the global economy, the increase in intra-industrial trade between Brazil and Argentina is heartening, even though this process started before 1991 when Mercosur was instituted (OECD, 1998). Table 4-6 shows the extent of intra-industry trade in 1992.

Table 4-7 traces the progress of intra-industrial trade by major sector between 1992 and 1996 using an intra-industry trade index that distinguishes between bilateral flows between Brazil and Argentina and trade flows with nonmember countries. The trade index is stable in the chemical and related products sector; it increased in the mechanical and transportation equipment sector and in the Standard International Trade Classification (SITC) manufacturing sectors 6 & 8—revealing a mature pattern of trade among members (Markwald and Machado, 1999). While it may be too soon to expect a full flowering of Mercosur's potential, there is room for cautious optimism regarding trade integration in the alliance.

Transport margins on intramember trade including Chile are lower than those on trade with Europe and North America, especially trade with the two large countries (Brazil and Argentina) by about 6 percentage points. This 6 percent margin is viewed as a rather small advantage to intraregional trade in view of the policy-based barriers to trade in Mercosur (Amjadi and Winters, 1997). While geographic proximity may, in theory, confer a cost advantage, several other transport system attributes will affect transport costs. For example, in marine transport where terminal costs are much higher than freight rates, a shorter distance may lead to greater transport costs. Second, transport cost increases stem from a lack of sophistication and the low physical and human capital intensity of transit facilitation services (poor transport connectors, deficient information systems, underdeveloped risk mechanisms, unreformed customs and other border procedures, and the quality of a variety of other transit facilitation services). Third, a substantial cost increase may

Table 4-7. Intra-industry Trade Index for Mercosur Partners, 1992–96

					Trade within Mercosur (bilateral trade, Brazil–Argentina)					
			1996 trade			Intra-industry trade indicator				
			Value	Share						
SITC[a]	Description		(US$ billions)	(percent)	1992	1993	1994	1995	1996
5	Chemical and related products		1.16	9.8	61	46	50	57	62
6	Manufactured goods classified by raw material		1.68	14.1	17	22	27	42	46
7	Mechanical and transportation equipment		4.14	34.7	41	58	65	73	66
8	Other manufactured articles		0.43	3.6	36	29	33	60	62

a. Standard industrial trade classification.
Source: Markwald and Machado (1999, 71).

derive from the inefficiencies of (frequently state-owned) transport and telecommunications monopolies.

Mercosur countries are rapidly improving their trade-transport chain to lower such costs. Chile is organizing itself along with its Asian and Pacific competitors for Electronic Data Interchange (EDI). Other countries lag behind in trade facilitation and domestic EDI, except for Brazil. Prompted by its history of explosive inflation, Brazil has developed electronic banking and a financial EDI user base. Private sector agencies and industry bodies in Brazil are beginning to develop business systems EDI. Schware and Kimberley (1995) suggest that Brazil can create an effective trade-transport chain by building upon its financial information technology base. To accomplish this objective, Brazil needs an appropriate legal framework, a shared vision within the public sector of electronic commerce, and collaboration and reform of its activities by customs and other public sector agencies to facilitate seamless cross-border freight flow.

Improvements in transport infrastructure lower transport costs. The newly constructed railway between Argentina and Brazil is expected to double transport capacity and save considerable time, with a 40 percent lowering of costs. The increase in investments in highways, railroads, and ports that has accompanied recent transportation privatization efforts in Argentina and other countries is fueling the expansion of transport capacity.

Transport Privatization and Deregulation

Transport service liberalization and deregulation—a necessary precursor to an efficient trade-transport chain—occurred in the 1990s in Mercosur countries. They were propelled by the inability of their publicly offered transport services to improve operational efficiency and services, to arrest cost increases, to attract new investment, to achieve quality maintenance, or to lower public subsidies. Transport industries— along with other industries such as telecommunications and utilities— were privatized to varying degrees in member countries. Argentina was one of the leaders in privatization. During the early 1990s, it sold off various public enterprises, including the Aerolineas Argentinas (one of the largest airlines in Latin America), railroads, and important turnpikes. Brazilian railways were privatized more recently and lag behind the liberalization efforts of their Argentine counterparts (Zinn, 1999).

Transport Privatization in Argentina

Argentina, together with Chile and Mexico, went farther than most Latin American countries in liberalizing various parts of the transport sector.[1] Unlike in the power and telecommunications sectors, which were sold outright, Argentina granted transport concessions of ten to thirty years, with ownership and control of assets returning to the government at the end of the concession. The concession dealt with the problems that motivated privatization without limiting the government's future options or flexibility. Further, concession contracts in rail transport (which is a "natural monopoly") must be carefully prepared in order to avoid complex regulatory structures.[2]

Ferrocarriles Argentinos (FA), the state-owned railroad company, was broken up into three different components—freight, intercity passenger, and commuter rail—and privatized in that order. Of the 31,000-kilometer freight rail network, 23,000 kilometers were viewed as commercially viable. (The rest was offered to provincial governments to take up or to abandon.) The 23,000 kilometers were offered as separate concessions— mostly in separate corridors radiating out of Buenos Aires. Table 4-8 lists five of these rail freight concessions that went into effect in 1993.

Although the busy Buenos Aires–Mar del Plata intercity passenger line garnered four bids, it was temporarily operated by the provincial government during preparation for future offers of private concessions. Most of the remaining intercity rail passenger services were abandoned. Ferrocarriles Argentinos's 900-kilometer urban commuter railroad that centered on Buenos Aires (1 million passengers a day) and the municipally owned subway system (0.5 million riders per day) were privatized.

The intercity highway system—about 9,830 kilometers that averaged at least a daily traffic volume of 2,000 to 2,500 vehicles per day—was offered up as concessions. The concessionaires could levy tolls in return for undertaking a specified program of maintenance and capacity enhancements (table 4-9). A similar concessions program for improving major access roads of major metropolitan areas was added.

In the early 1990s, many of the restrictive regulations and laws governing working practices at ports and waterways and on vessels were abolished. Before then Argentine port and waterway shipping charges were among the highest in the world for the poor services of a public agency. Special new port authorities composed of governments and shippers were created, and port terminals were leased as concessions.

A major consequence of rail privatization was savings in railroad subsidies, which had averaged US$1.4 billion annually in the 1980s. After privatization, the new private intercity freight companies received no subsidies, while the urban commuter and subway concessionaires were to receive an average of less than $100 million per year over twelve years.

---

1. This section is based on Gomez-Ibanez (1997).

2. The government established specialized regulatory agencies to stage the competition, carry out final contractual negotiations, and monitor and enforce contracts.

Table 4-8. Winning Bids of Rail Freight Concessions

Concession	Length (kilometers)	Private concessionaire	Date of takeover	Number of bids	Promised fee to government[a]	Invest-ments[a]	Jobs to Ferrocarriles Argentinos workers Number	Percent	Demand projections (millions of tons) Year 1	Year 2
Rosario-Bahia Blanca	5,163	Ferroexpresso Pampeano (FEPSA)	November 1, 1991	2	48.4	234	1,500	85	3.4	6.1
Mitre	4,520	Nuevo Central Argentino (NCA)	December 23, 1992	2	33.5	386	2,322	78	4.2	7.9
San Martin	5,493	Buenos Aires al Pacifico (BAP)	August 26, 1993	2	36.4	369	2,271	83	2.9	4.7
Urquiza	2,751	Ferrocarril Mesopotamico	October 22, 1993	1	2.8	64	1,255	76	0.9	1.9
Roca	4,791	Ferrosur Roca	March 12, 1993	1	18	173	1,133	86	2.7	6.4
Total	22,781				139.1	1,226	6,912	82	14.1	27.0

Note: Investments are for first fifteen years only.

a. Millions of U.S. dollars.

Source: Gomez-Ibanez (1997).

Table 4-9. Intercity Highway Concessions

Corridor	Concessionaire	Length (kilometers)	Number of toll booths	Basic toll range November, 1994 (U.S. dollars per vehicle)
1	Semacar, S.A.	665	3	2.6–3.3
2	Semacar, S.A.	297	2	1.8–1.9
3	Caminos del Oeste, S.A.	508	3	2.1–2.5
4	Caminos del Oeste, S.A.	697	3	2.5–3.1
5	Nuevos Rutas, S.A.	421	2	2.6
6	Covico, U.T.E.	479	3	1.2–3.4
7	Servicios Viales, S.A.	242	2	2.5–2.6
8	Servicios Viales, S.A.	694	3	1.9–2.5
9	Servicios Viales, S.A.	298	2	1.5
10	Covicentro, S.A.	332	2	1.9–2.1
11	Covinorte, S.A.	714	3	2.6–3.1
12	Concanor, S.A.	481	3	2.1
13	Virgen de Itati, S.A.	946	6	1.2–3.3
14	Rutas del Valle, S.A.	280	2	1.8
16	Camino del Abra, S.A.	404	3	1.2–2.4
17	Nuevas Rutas, S.A.	540	3	2.2–2.3
18	Caminos del Rio Uruguay, S.A.	618	4	1.6–4.1
20	Red Vial; Centro, S.A.	309	4	1.0–1.6

Source: Gomez-Ibanez (1997).

These savings derived from a combination of increased labor productivity and abandonment of lightly used (intercity passenger) services and lines. Ridership increased between 1993 and 1994 in urban commuter rail (45 percent) and subway (18 percent). The freight volume reached the levels of the 1980s, but some of the freight lines had difficulties stemming from the intense competition from truck services, which were helped by geography and public policy. Since the average lengths of haul were relatively short (500 kilometers), trucks could compete with the six rail networks that also overlapped. The tax field was not level: the diesel fuel used by heavy trucks was not taxed and gasoline was heavily taxed. Furthermore, rail companies had to lower rates in response to truckers doing so. All this affected adversely rail revenues and their potential for investment and track maintenance. There is concern that freight concessionaires were disinvesting in the networks, thereby lowering speeds (for intercity passenger service) and service levels (Gomez-Ibanez, 1997).

The physical condition of the privatized highways has improved significantly, and the cost of maintenance was moved off the government budget. However, there is no direct evidence that the cost of road maintenance is lower for the private sector (Gomez-Ibanez, 1997). Road usage has climbed, partly due to road improvements and mainly from economic recovery.

The mix of privatization and deregulation in ports and waterways sharply dropped port charges and barge and ocean shipping tariffs. Shipping costs for containers from Argentina to northern Europe fell from 30 percent to 70 percent between 1991 and 1993; for grain and bulk shipments, a savings of 10 percent materialized. The savings were largely derived from increasing labor productivity. Employment at the ports of Buenos Aires fell from the pre-privatization level of 8,000 to 2,500. The concession for the Atlantic Ocean–Santa Fe waterway was expected to maintain the channel at less cost than the public agency had spent, while obliged to maintain deeper channel depth North of Buenos Aires (Gomez-Ibanez, 1997).

Transport Infrastructure

Although Mercosur countries have rail networks extensive enough to offer a major mode for freight shipments, the service potential is hampered by the rail network's multiple gauges—not only between countries but within countries. This nonstandardization of gauges leads to costly transshipments. Zinn (1999) notes that this barrier has led in one case to an intermodal innovation: Interferra, a firm operating railroads in Argentina and Brazil, is planning to link the petrochemical-producing region in Salvador (Brazil) to Pacific ports in Chile using road railers (cars with both rail and truck wheels). Although road railers have a lower capacity than a regular rail car, they can easily be converted from rail to road carrier and vice versa.

However, motor carriers dominate freight traffic in Mercosur—90 percent according to Zinn (1999). This dominance reflects the superior road network in Argentina and Brazil, which have emphasized highway construction and the development of the automobile industry since the 1950s. The high quality of motor transport equipment, maintenance, labor, and infrastructure maintenance services contributes to the dominance of motor carrier transportation in Mercosur. As a consequence, in Mercosur even low-value cargo typically moved by water or rail (such as grains and minerals) is moved by motor carrier in member countries.

The inland waterway system known as the Paraguay-Parana system offers an economical alternative to transporting low-value bulk cargo by trucks. The Paraguay River runs from western Brazil through the Sao Paulo state to the Argentine border where it merges with the Parana River with links to the Atlantic Ocean via the port of Buenos Aires. This

Table 4-10. Selected Indicators of Transport within Mercosur, by Country, 1996, 1997

Country	Rail freight (kilometer ton per millions of dollars of GNP)[a]		Air passengers, 1996 (thousands)
	1996	1997	
Argentina	36,412		7,913
Bolivia	37,118		1,784
Brazil	56,068		22,012
Chile	15,882	5,998	3,633
Paraguay			261
Uruguay	10,455	16,125	504

a. In purchasing power parity.
Source: World Bank (2000b, 264).

waterway system, located at the center of a vast region accounting for 30 percent of the GDP, transports the regional agricultural commodities and minerals—increasing the region's trade more than twelve times in ten years (Zinn, 1999). If appropriate dredging and lock systems around dams are completed, these types of freight can move from Compinas (sixty miles West of Sao Paulo) to Buenos Aires at *half* the cost of truck transportation.

The differences in the technical standards for truck sizes between Argentina (59 feet) and Brazil (60 feet, 8 inches) represented a harmonization problem. When Mercosur adopted the 59-ft. standard, the Brazilian truck fleet was disadvantaged (Zinn, 1999). Table 4-10 displays selected indicators of transport performance within Mercosur.

Transport Integration and Activity Restructuring

As the transport and transit facilitation systems improve in Mercosur, the direct effects of improvement—in terms of a virtuous cycle of lower costs, increasing trade volume, and economies of scale and scope in distribution and production activities—set in motion adaptive responses by various economic agents in the trade bloc. These agents—producers, shippers, carriers, distributors, and other facilitators—begin to see Mercosur as an integrated market rather than as a set of separate markets, and they reconfigure their activities accordingly. It is during this restructuring and rationalization of production and distribution activities that further economies of scale and scope can emerge to continue the virtuous loop. Such long-term consequences represent the full benefits of trade liberalization and a supportive trade-transport chain.

Some large North American corporations that operate global production and distribution networks have seized the integration opportunities offered by Mercosur and begun to integrate their prior nation-based activities into a Mercosur-wide framework. The rest of this chapter briefly describes the future-oriented supply chain systems developed in Mercosur by Kodak and Kellogg (Zinn 1999). Supply chains represent a network of firms that carry out production, distribution, and other supporting activities that link the producer and the consumer.

Kodak: Multicountry Warehousing from a Single Location

Taking advantage of the rise of the Mercosur trading bloc, Kodak has integrated its once separate national warehousing operations into a trade-bloc-wide operation. Now it distributes its high-value, low-volume, and low-weight products to one large market (Mercosur and Peru) supplied from a single warehouse in Brazil. The major advantages of a multi-country facility derive from economies of scale in distribution and the resultant cost savings from higher volumes and from the more efficient use of transportation assets, warehousing equipment, and software. Furthermore, a single large location can offer the customer a high level of stock availability per inventory investment. Zinn (1999) notes another reason for Kodak's choice of a location in Brazil (the largest national market)—a tax incentive Brazil offers for imported products earmarked for re-export.

Kodak was able to increase its negotiating leverage by consolidating shipments to fewer oceanic ports. In addition, the cost of supporting the expansion of Kodak's business into new markets is lowered when products are supplied from a centralized facility.

The feasibility of Kodak's strategy of a single facility for a trade bloc is clearly contingent on a seamless trade-transport chain. First, cost-effective transportation and complementary information must be available to serve a large market from a single location. Other barriers Kodak had to overcome include the high costs of operating through Brazilian ports (as compared to international levels), the excessive documentation burden, the longer cycle times at customs, which is not open 24 hours a day, and the delay-inducing propensity of multiple governmental agencies to work in sequence rather than in parallel. Only when such barriers are fully lowered in Brazil can smaller companies with products of lower value/weight ratios than Kodak sells follow its strategy of trade-bloc-wide service from one warehouse.

Kellogg's: Integrated Supply Chains for Brazil and Argentina

Kellogg's—producing in Argentina and Brazil and importing from the United States, Mexico and South Africa—designed a supply chain for the joint Argentina-Brazil market. Such a supply chain's design depends on Mercosur-wide criteria for allocating production, a reasonably free flow of goods between Argentina and Brazil, and the extensive use of third-party logistics for local warehousing and distribution and for operating the main distribution centers (DCs) close to the largest markets of Sao Paulo and Buenos Aires. This chapter cannot do justice to this complex system. Instead, it will outline the types of obstacles to the efficient implementation of this supply chain in the Mercosur environment.

The key to success in the Kellogg's system is the speed, reliability, and the cost of shipment across the Brazil-Argentina border. The key obstacles are lack of harmonized documentation between Argentina and Brazil, tax legislation that makes it cheaper to serve customers from a more distant out-of-state warehouse than from an in-state warehouse, and the involvement of customs in every shipment on both sides of the border.

As more global and regional corporations develop similar transport chain innovations, greater operational efficiencies and lower transport costs will ensue in Mercosur. If at the same time, appropriate investments in transport and communication infrastructure take place and cross-border processes—customs, inspections, harmonizations of standards, and documentation—are reformed to world-class levels, Mercosur can look forward to the dawn of an era of seamless intrabloc trade and transport.

5

Southern African Development Community: The Maputo Corridor

William P. Anderson

The Southern African Development Community (SADC) was established in 1992 as a cooperative effort of the governments of Angola, Botswana, Lesotho, Malawi, Mozambique, Namibia, Swaziland, Tanzania, Zambia, and Zimbabwe. It grew out of a predecessor organization of Frontline States founded in 1981 to oppose and economically isolate the apartheid government of South Africa. With the political transformations in the region, South Africa became a member of SADC in 1994. This greatly changed the Community: South Africa in 1998 accounted for about 80 percent of its total GDP. During the late 1990s, the Democratic Republic of Congo and the Indian Ocean nations of Mauritius and Seychelles also joined the Southern African Development Community.

By 1998 the SADC states had a combined population of 180 million and a combined land area of 9 million square kilometers (Kaombwe, 1998). The states, asymmetrical economically because of the membership of South Africa, were heterogeneous in a number of other ways as well (table 5-1). The Southern African Development Community includes landlocked states (Swaziland, Lesotho, Botswana) and island nations (Mauritius and Seychelles). Per capita GDP is highest in the Indian Ocean states, and in the remaining states it varies from about $3,000 and $4,000 (Botswana, South Africa) to roughly $200 or less (Malawi, Mozambique, Democratic Republic of Congo). Some states (Angola, Namibia, and Swaziland) are highly trade dependent. Mozambique is notable for its low level of exports, despite its maritime location. All except Mauritius and Seychelles form a contiguous mass occupying the southern third of the African continent.

The objectives of SADC include economic and social development and the alleviation of poverty; promotion of economic and political

Table 5-1. Financial Profile of the Southern African Development Community, by Country, 1998

Country	Population (millions)	Population growth rate, 1992–98	GNP (billions of U.S. dollars)	GDP per capita (U.S. dollars)	Exports[a] as percentage of GDP	Imports[a] as percentage of GDP
Angola	12.0	3.1	4.1	340	57.1	69.0
Botswana	1.6	2.4	5.6	3,600	35.0	33.8
Democratic Rep. of Congo	48.2	3.2	5.3	110	23.8	22.0
Lesotho	2.1	2.2	1.2	570	33.5	124.7
Malawi	10.5	2.6	2.1	200	32.5	45.6
Mauritius	1.2	1.1	4.3	3,700	64.8	65.0
Mozambique	16.9	2.4	3.6	210	11.7	24.2
Namibia	1.7	2.6	3.2	1,940	63.1	63.3
Seychelles	0.08	1.5	0.51	6,450	67.1	77.4
South Africa	41.3	2.0	119.0	2,880	25.8	24.5
Swaziland	1.0	3.1	1.4	1,400	101.5	94.6
Zambia	9.7	2.6	3.2	330	29.4	38.4
Zimbabwe	11.6	2.6	6.4	610	40.3	41.7

a. Of goods and services.

Source: "At a Glance," World Bank web site, www.worldbank.org/data/countrydata/countrydata.html.

liberties; peace and security; and regional economic integration. With the end of apartheid in 1994 and the end of the civil war in Mozambique in 1993, the opportunity for SADC to focus its attention on economic integration as a means of promoting development goals improved. Given the relative youth of the Community, the weak economic ties among member states, the lack of a strong tradition for economic cooperation, and the poor condition of international transportation and communication infrastructure, it is still at a very early stage of development as a trade bloc.

One area where significant strides are being made is in the establishment (or reestablishment) of transportation infrastructure corridors connecting member states—especially connections between South Africa and other states. While these strides are largely the outcome of bilateral rather than Community-wide agreements, they are an important prerequisite for increased regional integration. The corridors are being developed along the lines for policy harmonization established under the 1996 SADC Transport Protocol, which stressed the need for private sector participation and the role of transportation in economic integration. The most ambitious of the corridor projects is the Maputo Development Corridor (MDC), created in 1995.

The Maputo Development Corridor

Trade blocs in affluent parts of the world face the problem of integrating and facilitating movement across existing infrastructure systems. By contrast, trade blocs in developing regions are faced with an absolute shortage of infrastructure—especially cross-border infrastructure. Major cross-border infrastructure initiatives in these trade blocs serve the dual role of supporting increased trade between countries and promoting economic development along infrastructure-rich corridors within countries. One such initiative is the Maputo Development Corridor.

The MDC is a joint effort by the governments of South Africa and Mozambique, both members of the Southern African Development Community. Rather than blazing a new trail, the MDC seeks to reestablish the once-vital corridor linking South Africa's inland industrial heartland around Johannesburg and the capacious Indian Ocean port of Maputo in southern Mozambique. This corridor had fallen into disuse and disrepair in the past few decades when political and military events precluded cooperation and trade between the two countries.

The Maputo Development Corridor has the obvious benefit of linking an established industrial region inland with its most advantageous outlet to foreign markets. The goals behind the MDC initiative, however, are much broader. It is hoped that the MDC will promote new types of economic development in areas where economic prospects have been limited by poor accessibility to resources and markets. Thus, MDC is a prime example of the *development corridor concept*, which plays an increasing role in the economic strategies of low- and middle-income regions.

The Development Corridor Concept

The poor state of transport corridors linking marine ports with interior regions severely limits growth prospects in many low-income countries. This is especially true in Africa, where many of the regions with the greatest development potential—that is, regions with rich resource bases—are located in the interior, and the general state of roads and rail there is poor and often deteriorating. Since most African economies are not very diversified, imports of fuels, chemicals, spare parts, and material are often critical to economic development. This problem is greatest for land-locked countries because national infrastructure systems are not well integrated, border procedures are inefficient, and regional conflicts often rule out cross-border shipments. For many critical industrial inputs, c.i.f. (cost, insurance, freight) prices may be 50 to 70 percent higher than f.o.b. (free on board) prices, and there are long delays in goods delivery attributable primarily to the overland segments of shipments (World

Bank, 1995). Naturally this increases production costs and delays in getting products to international markets, and it reduces the competitiveness of local producers. Improvement in coast-to-interior corridors is an important precondition for export-driven development.

This is only part of the story because it only takes account of activities occurring at opposite ends of the corridor. In affluent countries there are many examples of concentrated economic development occurring along the length of a corridor. Examples include industrial regions extending along waterways such as the Ruhr in Germany or along highways such as the Route 128 high-technology corridor in the United States. Furthermore, such corridors may straddle international borders. An example is the automotive production region concentrated along major highways; it extends from the U.S. Great Lake States into the Canadian province of Ontario and produces the largest cross-border flow of goods in the world.

In such cases economic vitality is enhanced not only by improved accessibility to external resources and markets but also by high levels of accessibility *within* the corridor. Ease of interaction among firms leads to efficient movement of intermediate goods, rapid diffusion of technological and market information, and the evolution of skilled and specialized labor forces upon which new firms can draw.

The development corridor concept essentially seeks to reproduce this pattern of highly integrated and self-reinforcing growth in low- or middle-income countries. The development corridor is defined as that area in the vicinity of a new infrastructure route "spine" (Development Bank of Southern Africa, 1998). This spine may be a highway, rail line, or even a pipeline or electric transmission corridor, but ideally it will comprise an integrated system of some or all of these infrastructure elements supported by a modern communications system. Within this corridor imported inputs will be cheaper, access to international markets will be better, interconnections among firms will be stronger, the movement of labor resources will be freer, and the diffusion of innovations will be faster. The hope is that economic development will be fostered not only at opposite ends of the corridor but throughout its length.

History and Context of MDC

As late as 1975, the port of Maputo was the main outlet to international trade for the industrial region around Johannesburg. Both road and rail links were established on an East-West orientation, extending mostly across the South African province of Mpumalanga and also across the southern Maputo province of Mozambique, which includes the port. The economic isolation of the apartheid government and the civil war in Mozambique made this link impractical, and shipments were diverted to a more expensive route via Natal. As a result, Maputo port volumes fell from 11 million tons in 1975 to 1.6 million tons in the mid-1980s. They recovered to more than 3 million tons in the late 1990s (von Klaudy, 1999b).

Reestablishment of the traditional transport link is clearly in the interest of both countries, since it would increase the competitiveness of industries currently operating in South Africa and return substantial revenues to the port of Maputo. Furthermore, in line with the development corridor concept, reestablishment of the transport "spine" has the potential to promote development outside the traditional industries and locations in both countries. Through years of neglect and disuse, however, the main elements of the infrastructure, especially in Mozambique, had become inadequate for the task. A major investment project was needed to reestablish the link. In 1995 the transport ministers of South Africa and Mozambique agreed to a massive infrastructure project to rehabilitate, and in some cases rebuild, the road and rail infrastructure system along the Maputo Corridor extending from Witbank in South Africa to the port of Maputo.

The corridor serves areas of South Africa with high development potential but with severe problems of poverty, unemployment, and misallocation of population. In the 1990s more than 65 percent of the gross provincial product of the Mpumalanga province was contributed by the mining, manufacturing, and electric, gas, and water sectors. However, the population of the province is largely rural and unevenly distributed. Forty percent of the people of Mpumalanga are crowded into the former homeland areas, which occupy only 10 percent of the land. Thirty percent live in formal urban areas, which are the location of most industrial employment, but a growing number are migrating from the countryside to informal urban areas with limited development opportunities. Unemployment in the province reached more than 17 percent in the 1990s. The province is well endowed with natural resources, allowing many new avenues for development. Many of the resources are exported in the form of raw materials, with relatively little fabrication or processing (Development Bank of Southern Africa, 1998).

Maputo province, which includes the city and port of Maputo, has more than 50 percent of the Mozambican population. This share increased substantially during the civil war as people fled the northern rural areas. The provincial economy, dominated by manufacturing and service activities, has been unable to absorb the rapid growth in the labor force. Unemployment ballooned in the 1990s to over 20 percent compared with a national rate of around 8 percent (Development Bank of Southern Africa, 1998).

Thus, both the Maputo province and Mpumalanga province are in need of new urban economic activities to absorb an already concentrated and underemployed population. Their development advantages are complementary: Mpumalanga has a rich resource base, while Maputo has good accessibility to world markets. In general, the potential development advantages provided by the corridor include:

- Reductions in the cost and time delay of transportation within South Africa and Mozambique, and with world markets;
- Economies of scale through aggregation of resources distributed throughout the corridor;
- Vertical integration through interactions among firms in complementary activities along the corridor;
- Access to new international markets, such as the market for fresh produce in the Middle East and the growing world tourism market (Development Bank of Southern Africa, 1998).

In order to achieve these advantages in a way that would benefit the population and be within reasonable fiscal bounds, the agreement between South Africa and Mozambique stated four goals:

- To enhance and where necessary rehabilitate the transport infrastructure from Witbank to Maputo on the basis of a public sector–private sector partnership;
- To maximize investment in the corridor area and to ensure that the sustainable growth and development that arises therefrom is adequately supported by integrated infrastructure development;
- To maximize the social development impact of investment in the Maputo Development Corridor, particularly to disadvantaged communities;
- To ensure environmental sustainability of the project by developing policies, strategies, and frameworks that encompass a holistic, participatory, and integrated approach to environmental management (Development Bank of Southern Africa, 1998).

The last two goals reflect the concern that the MDC should not merely reproduce past economic patterns based on export-oriented resource extraction yielding highly inequitable benefits and with the potential of severe environmental degradation.

Plan, Operation, and Potential Benefits

The MDC project has four major transportation infrastructure components: upgrading and construction of road link from Witbank to Maputo; improvement of rail service from Johannesburg to Maputo, along with lines connecting Maputo to Zimbabwe and Swaziland; upgrading port and harbor operations in Maputo; and establishment of a modern, integrated border post to speed movements between South Africa and Mozambique. The transportation components of the project are complemented by the upgrading of telecommunications systems in the corridor, programs to enhance development of small and medium enterprises, and the promotion of major industrial projects in the corridor.

The toll road is being developed under a concession contract signed in May 1997 between the two governments and Trans African Concessions (TRAC), a private sector consortium owned largely by two South African road contractors and the international construction firm Bouygues. Under the contract, TRAC takes responsibility for the design, construction, rehabilitation, financing, operation, and maintenance of the toll road. Thus broad responsibilities—along with considerable financial risk—are ceded to a private sector partner. Most of the new construction is on the Mozambique end of the road. The concession contract includes construction of a new border post at Ressano Garcia / Komatipoort (Trans African Concessions, n.d.). The total cost of the toll road is about US$320 million.

As of mid-2000 the road project was on schedule for completion by the end of the year. The newly constructed segment in Mozambique was scheduled to open in August 2000. The construction has created 4,700 permanent, casual, and temporary jobs, many of which are for persons trained in special constructions schools set up by Trans African Concessions.[1] Construction of the border post, which is critical to providing effective road service, has been delayed because of disagreements among government agencies in South Africa.

Progress on rail and port improvements has been slower than on road improvements. The rail corridor within South Africa was already well established, so the improvements are largely in Mozambique. Port and rail operations in Mozambique are currently operated by the state organization Portos e Caminhos de Ferro de Mocambique (CFM). The plan, however, is to make three concession contracts with private groups to operate rail-port systems. These include rail links to Swaziland and Zimbabwe as well as to South Africa. Negotiations are under way with potential concessionaires, and one concession for the rail line to Ressano Garcia (along the main spine of the MDC) is in place. The process has experienced considerable delays, which are attributable in part to the poor state of Mozambique's infrastructure and government institutions as a result of the civil war.

---

1. Stephan K. L. von Klaudy, memo regarding minutes of team meeting December 6, 1999: "End-of-Millenium Update on Corridor Projects and Developments." The World Bank.

Besides the toll road, the most important development in the corridor is the Mozal aluminum smelter in Maputo, which has been built at a cost of US$1.4 billion by South African and British interests. This facility began producing aluminum for export in June 2000, and this will have a massive effect on Mozambique's balance of trade. Power is supplied from sources in South Africa. Another massive metals project in the planning state is the Maputo Iron and Steel Plant (MISP) that would exploit natural gas from the Pande fields in Mozambique. There is still, however, uncertainty as to whether this project will go forward.[2]

It remains to be seen whether more modest and spatially distributed economic development benefits will come about as the transportation infrastructure elements come into service. Despite the mineral wealth of the South African interior, only very basic iron and steel production occurs. There are no facilities to produce the cold-rolled steel that is used in various fabricated metal and other manufacturing industries. The Development Bank of Southern Africa (1998) has suggested that with improved transportation services it may be possible to develop a complex of higher value-added steel-based industries within the corridor, rather than exporting the steel in a relatively raw form. The same applies to other minerals-based industries. However, such development will require significant progress in skills enhancement and support for the establishment of small and medium-size enterprises.

Even rural areas might benefit from a shift to agricultural products that are more highly valued on international markets. Both the Mpumalanga province and the Maputo province have appropriate agricultural resources for the production of fresh fruits and vegetables that could be exported through the port of Maputo to markets in the Middle East (Development Bank of Southern Africa, 1998). This naturally would require a high level of performance along the entire transportation corridor, including rapid border crossings and port operations. Development along these lines would go a long way toward meeting the goal of extending the benefits of the MDC to a broader segment of the population.

Tourism is another area in which transportation infrastructure development may support rapid growth. Tourism is already a major boon to the economy of the Mpumalanga province, contributing 14 percent of total employment. More than one million visitors are attracted every year, especially to the lowveld area, and annual growth exceeds 10 percent. Tourism growth in Mozambique was precluded during the war period, but today some believe that the coastal areas could become the most important tourist zone in southern Africa (Development Bank of

---

2. Ibid.

Southern Africa, 1998). High-quality transportation and communication could make it possible to provide packaged tours of the two areas.

Institutional Problems

The MDC initiative began in 1995 and is still ongoing; most of the highway infrastructure project was completed by mid-year 2000, with the remaining elements slated for completion by the end of the year. Thus far, progress is impressive. There are, however, a number of areas where proposed activities are either behind schedule or are failing to meet expectations. For the most part, these problems stem more from inadequate institutional arrangements than from technological or logistical difficulties.

Some of these problems reflect the asymmetry of population size, level of affluence, and business sector experience between Mozambique and South Africa. Both the public and private sectors in Mozambique fear that the benefits from the MDC, in terms of construction contracts and economic development, will accrue disproportionately to South African firms. Indeed, the Maputo Corridor Company, which was envisioned in 1995 as a jointly managed enterprise to manage corridor activities, was never implemented by Mozambique.[3]

Others problems arise from the inefficient state of Mozambican institutions after a long period of warfare. For example, rail and port development in Mozambique will involve a transfer of the activities of CFM to private concessionaires, who will surely operate with a much smaller labor force, leading to massive redundancy among CFM's employees. Making the transition in a way that minimizes the blow to displaced workers is a major challenge in the contracting process. Moreover, a recent study (Linfield, 1999) concluded that the institutional structure put in place by both countries for the MDC is ill suited to the task.

In addition to the development and rehabilitation of transport facilities, the investment priorities of MDC include:

- Upgrading water, sanitation, health care, and education in low-income communities;
- Provision of local roads and footpaths to increase accessibility within the corridor;
- Provision of infrastructure for developing industrial areas such as drainage, water, and waste disposal; and
- Environmental interventions such as coastal zone management and fuelwood management.

---

3. Ibid.

Broad responsibility for the Maputo Development Corridor was given to the Transport Ministries, and their expertise in these areas is limited. The structure of oversight and management is dominated by federal government officials, despite a move toward devolution of transport and development-related activities to the municipal and provincial levels of government. Thus, the ability to implement plans is severely retarded.

Some institutional reform has already occurred. In South Africa responsibility for the MDC was transferred from the Department of Transport to the Department of Trade and Industry, which has incorporated MDC into its Spatial Development Initiative programs. A more novel institutional development is the Borderlands Committee (BC), created in 1998. It includes representatives of provincial and local governments. Swaziland, which had previously been left out of MDC decisionmaking despite its proximity to the corridor, also participates. The Borderlands Committee has actively promoted issues of local concern to the corridor, including border facilitation along the lines of the SADC Protocol, environmental management, and development of tourism and other services.

The Maputo Development Corridor, despite the foregoing institutional problems, exemplifies successful international cooperation within the SADC to promote mutual economic benefit and, in time, greater economic integration. The main thrust of this initiative has been the creation of *physical infrastructure systems*. Without them, integrated, diversified, equitable, and sustainable economic development is impossible. The ultimate success of the MDC, however, may well depend upon the ability to develop *nonphysical infrastructure* such as smooth border operations, good business logistics systems, and other knowledge and competencies in transportation and trade facilitation.

6

Transport, Logistics, and Trade Facilitation in the South Asia Subregion

Uma Subramanian

Recent trends in globalization, supported by technological advances in information, communication, and transportation, have decentralized production and distribution activities worldwide. This decentralization process offers economic opportunities to all countries, particularly developing countries, by allowing them to provide value added services and low-cost raw material or human resource skills. In turn, these countries benefit from improved market access for their exports, acquisition of knowledge and new technology through international transfers, efficiency gains in the economy resulting from increased competitive pressures on domestic economic activities, and greater employment opportunities. The ability of countries to grow rapidly depends on their capacity to link with global and regional markets. In turn, this capacity depends on connectivity and the efficiency and speed with which goods and services can be moved from production centers to final markets, ensuring high-quality and "just in time" delivery in response to market demand. These are important parameters in the emerging global market where market expectations have risen substantially in the past few years.

Within regions or countries, efficient transport and logistics systems offer new possibilities for linking isolated and landlocked regions to markets, developing the resource base, integrating manufacturing and service activities across borders, and increasing employment. By facilitating access to a larger regional market, they could help countries benefit from economies of scale. By providing market access to rural areas, they enable rural producers and small industries to deliver quality products within an acceptable time and at a competitive cost. These changes have significant implications for opening up South Asia, one of the poorest regions in the world.

Ready-made garments and carpets, Nepal's top export commodities, have markets in Europe and the United States. Bangladesh's primary export, garments and knitwear, are transported to U.S. markets. Bhutan and Nepal are seeking regional markets for agricultural products in Bangladesh and India. The northeastern Indian states' horticultural products are currently confined to local markets or informally traded across borders for low prices but could find markets in Bangladesh. Similarly, the northeastern states of India could obtain fish, for instance, from Bangladesh instead of having fish transported from other Indian states (for example, Andhra Pradesh, West Bengal). The Indo-Bangladesh trade groups as well as policy research groups in the countries have identified the possibility for collaborative ventures in fertilizer, cement, and gas-based industries.[1]

As the South Asian countries position themselves to participate in global markets and strengthen their regional markets, transport costs and time must be reduced. Logistics inefficiencies translate into higher priced commodities and weaken these countries' credibility and position in the global market.

In discussions of regional transport and logistics systems, this fundamental question is often asked: to what extent does the economy of the transit country benefit from improvements in transport and logistics systems? The country providing the transport infrastructure could, in principle, recover its investment through appropriate charges to the transit vehicles and cargo while deriving additional value added from complementary services provided to these transport activities. The value added is the greatest where the transit country provides an efficient international seaport gateway and some of the trucking or rail services used in the logistics chain.

A more critical question of direct relevance to South Asia is frequently asked: to what extent do transport-logistics improvements benefit the poorer members of society? Benefits to them would derive from better access to domestic and foreign markets for local products and from the employment associated with upgrading the transport infrastructure. The medium- and long-term benefits are the continuity and even expansion of employment in economic activities or industries that, without better logistics, would not have been established or would rapidly lose market share. The extent and allocation of benefits would be affected, of course, by the following:

---

1. *Indo-Bangladesh Dialogue: Economic and Trade Cooperation, 1995,* report on a meeting hosted by the Center for Policy Dialogue, Bangladesh, and the Center for Policy Research, India, as part of ongoing dialogue among nongovernmental and research groups.

- How well the isolated and landlocked regions are served
- How labor intensive the new economic activities are
- How the charges are structured (that is, who pays and who benefits)
- How efficient the logistic systems become that will help minimize the cost to the economy.

As South Asia looks outward toward global markets and greater trade and investment relationships within the region, it could benefit from the experiences of countries in other regional trade blocs such as the Common Market of the South (Mercado Comin del Sur or Mercosur), the North American Free Trade Agreement (NAFTA) signatories, and the Southern African Development Community (SADC). Rotterdam port is a successful hub that has maintained its position as one of the world's largest ports for four decades. There are clear lessons in Rotterdam's experience for managers of ports and airports in South Asia as they organize their trade and transport chains. [2]

This chapter focuses on transportation and logistics issues in a subregion of South Asia covering Bangladesh, Bhutan, Nepal, and eastern and northeastern India. In the profile of the subregion that follows, we present an overview of economic growth indicators (table 6-1) and socioeconomic indicators (table 6-2). Subsequent sections of this chapter highlight transportation and logistics issues in the subregion that not only affect intraregional trade but also international trade, with strong implications for economic growth and poverty alleviation.

Profile of the Subregion

The South Asia subregion covering Bangladesh, Nepal, Bhutan, and eastern and northeastern India is home to almost half a billion people and is among the most densely populated areas in the world. More than half the population lives on less than $1 a day, and socioeconomic indicators (such as infant mortality, life expectancy, and adult and female literacy) are among the lowest in the world. During the next twenty-five years this population is expected to double, exacerbating poverty, social tension, and environmental degradation unless strategies for encouraging faster economic growth are conceived and implemented.

Though the subregion has abundant natural resources in the form of minerals, water, and energy resources, they are largely untapped because of poor connectivity and inadequate access to markets. Both Nepal and Bhutan are landlocked countries, as are the seven northeastern

---

2. In this volume see chapters 2, 4, 5, and 8.

Table 6-1. Economic Growth Indicators, South Asia

Indicator	India	Bangladesh	Nepal	Bhutan
Area (thousands of square kilometers)	3,288	144	147	47
Population (millions)				
1980	687	87	14	n.a.
1998	980	126	23	0.8
Average annual growth rate (%), 1997–98	2.0	2.1	2.5	n.a.
GNP, 1998 (billions of U.S. dollars)	427.4	44.2	4.9	0.4
Average annual growth rate (%), 1997–98	6.2	5.9	2.7	8.2
GNP per capita, 1998 (U.S. dollars)	440	350	210	470
Average annual growth rate (%), 1997–98	4.3	3.2	0.3	6.8
GNP per capita at purchasing power parity (U.S. dollars)	2,071	1,330	1,079	1,446
Trade as percentage of GNP				
1970	8.0	17.0	13.0	n.a.
1998	25.0	33.0	58.0	n.a.

n.a. Not available.
Source: World Bank (1999).

Indian states. The northeastern region of India is connected to the rest of India by a narrow congested land corridor between Bangladesh and Nepal.[3] This landlocked region, a natural hinterland to Chittagong port, trades with the rest of India and the world through this congested strip of land.

The costs of transporting goods to and from the northeastern region are consequently high. According to the report of the Committee on Clause Seven of the 1990 Assam accord, Assam was spending almost as much in transporting essential commodities such as food-grain, fish, and edible oils from "mainland" India as the costs of the commodities (Verghese, 1996). Tea from Assam is shipped to Europe via Calcutta port. The transportation cost includes a trucking distance of more than 1,400 kilometers through the land corridor around Bangladesh to Calcutta port. The traditional tea route for Assamese tea via Chittagong port would

---

3. This corridor is known in the subregion as the "chicken's neck."

Table 6-2. Socioeconomic Indicators, South Asia Subregion

Area	GNP per capita, dollars, 1998	Percentage of population living on less than $1/day	Percentage of population living on less than $2/day	Infant mortality rate, per 1,000, 1997	Under-5 mortality rate, per 1,000, 1997	Life expectancy at birth, 1997	Illiteracy rate, for adults (age 15 and older), 1997 Males	Females
The Subregion								
India	430	47	87.5	71	88	63	33	61
Bangladesh	350	50.3	86.7	75	104	58	50	73
Nepal	210	n.a.	n.a.	83	117	57	44	79
Bhutan	430	n.a.	n.a.	63	n.a.	61	n.a.	n.a.
Other countries								
Indonesia	680	7.7	50.4	47	60	65	9	20
China	750	22.2	57.8	32	39	70	9	25
Argentina	8,970	n.a.	n.a.	22	24	73	3	4
Brazil	4,570	23.6	43.5	34	44	67	16	16
Burkina Faso	n.a.	n.a.	n.a.	99	169	44	n.a.	n.a.
Namibia	n.a.	n.a.	n.a.	65	101	56	n.a.	n.a.
Regions								
East Asia and Pacific	990	n.a.	n.a.	37	47	69	9	22
Latin America and Caribbean	3,940	n.a.	n.a.	32	41	70	12	14
Sub-Saharan Africa	480	n.a.	n.a.	91	147	51	34	50
South Asia	430	n.a.	n.a.	77	100	62	36	63

n.a. Not available.
Note: South Asia includes all the countries in South Asia as categorized in the *World Development Report.*
Sources: World Bank (1999c, 2000b).

cut the distance by almost 60 percent. Third-country trade for both Nepal and Bhutan is also routed through this corridor to Calcutta port with associated delays and costs.

Historically, South Asian countries have had restrictive trade policy regimes with stringent barriers, quantitative and tariff restrictions on trade, restrictions on foreign capital investments, and a predominant role of the public sector in the direct production of goods and services and in regulating the private sector. Consequently, the place of trade in national income has been low. Foreign direct investment flows to the South Asian region have risen in the past decade but are low compared with those to other regions in the world (figure 6-1).

The trade restrictions also applied to cross-border and regional trade, which explains why trade among India, Bangladesh, Nepal, and Bhutan has been traditionally low. Figure 6-2 presents regional exports as a percentage of total exports for selected regional trade blocs. The percentage of exports among countries within the South Asian Association for Regional Cooperation (SAARC) remained at or below 5 percent of total exports worldwide between 1980 and 1997. This pattern differs mark-

Figure 6-1. Foreign Direct Investment in Selected Regions, 1990 and 1997

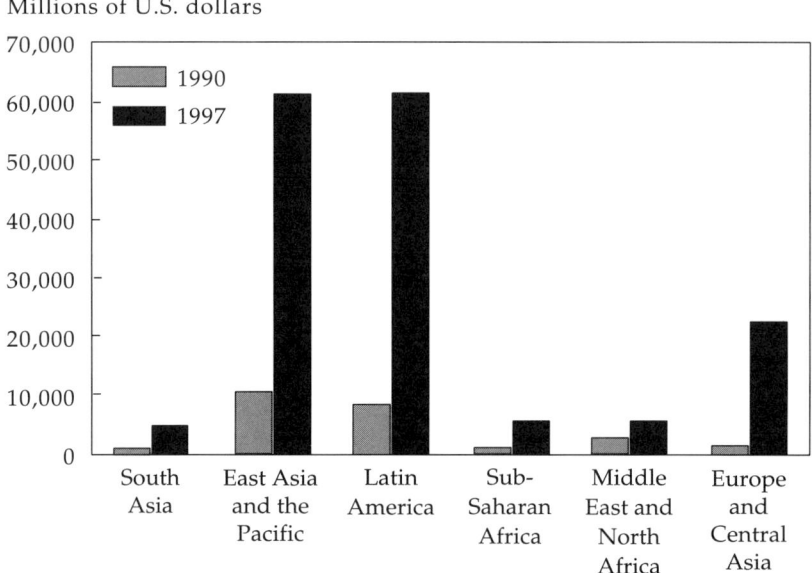

Millions of U.S. dollars

Source: World Bank (1999c).

Figure 6-2. Exports within Regional Trade Blocs as a Percentage of Total Exports, 1980–97

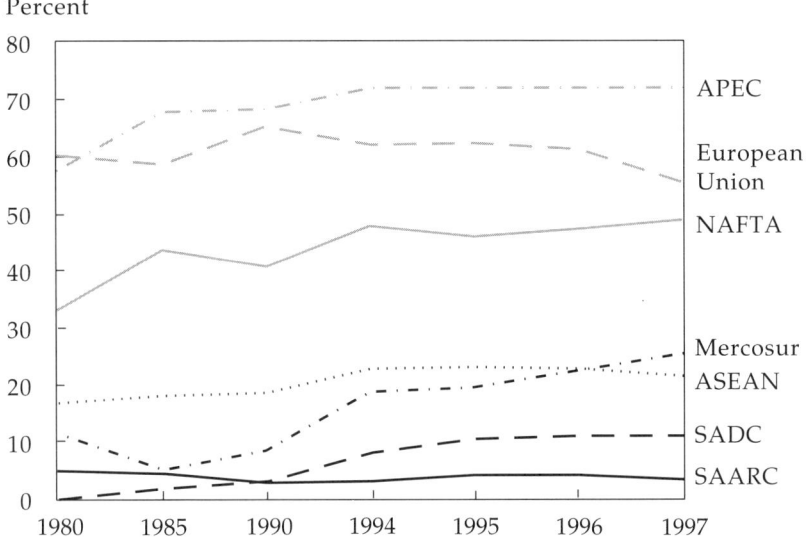

Note: The figure compares the exports within regional trade blocs as a percentage of total exports of the Asia-Pacific Economic Cooperation, the European Union, the North American Free Trade Agreement countries, the Common Market of the South (Mercado Comin del Sur or Mercosur), the Southern African Development Community, and the South Asian Association for Regional Cooperation.

Source: World Bank (1999c).

edly from other trade blocs such as Mercosur, NAFTA, and SADC. Intraregional exports within Mercosur and SADC were comparable to SAARC in 1985 but in the past fifteen years both trade blocs have increased intraregional exports by twofold or more. As seen in table 6-3, in all four countries intraregional trade is only a fraction of total third-country trade. Furthermore, this trade is concentrated in a few key commodities and demonstrates a significant level of dependence of the smaller countries on India. Table 6-4 shows the top ten commodities traded between India and Bangladesh in 1996, 1997, and 1998. For instance, textile yarn that dominates India's exports to Bangladesh is a primary raw material for Bangladesh's garment sector.

The low official intraregional trade is accompanied by significant informal trade among the countries concerned. It is estimated that unofficial exports from India to Bangladesh are approximately equal to official

Table 6-3. Intraregional Trade in South Asia, 1998

	Exports		Imports	
Intraregional trade	Millions of U.S. dollars[a]	Percentage of total exports	Millions of U.S. dollars[a]	Percentage of total imports
India's trade with				
Bangladesh	1,038	1.9	65	0.2
Nepal	324	0.6	147	0.5
Bhutan	12	0.0	15	0.1
Other countries	52,967	97.5	28,958	99.2
Total	54,341	100.0	29,185	100.0
Nepal's trade with				
India	146	32.9	440	30.7
Bangladesh	10	2.3	6	0.4
Bhutan	n.a.	0.0	n.a.	0.0
Other countries	288	64.9	988	68.9
Total	444	100.0	1,434	100.0
Bangladesh's trade with				
India	55	1.4	1,179	16.1
Nepal	18	0.5	14	0.2
Bhutan	n.a.	0.0	5	0.1
Other countries	3,749	98.1	6,115	83.6
Total	3,822	100.0	7,313	100.0
Bhutan's trade with				
India	11	9.4	9	6.6
Bangladesh	4	3.4	n.a.	0.0
Nepal	n.a.	0.0	n.a.	0.0
Other countries	102	87.2	128	93.4
Total	117	100.0	137	100.0

n.a. Not available.
Note: Data for 1998 Bhutan trade are not available. Therefore, data for 1997 are used.
a. Calculated based on an exchange rate of Ngultrum 36.313 to one U.S. dollar.
Sources: IMF (1999a, 1999b).

exports. A large portion of the unofficial exports (85 percent) is in the form of border trade between West Bengal and Bangladesh and consists mainly of food items, live animals (cattle), and consumer goods. The unofficial flow from Bangladesh into India is dominated by synthetic yarn, electronic goods, and spices. A sizable percentage (44 percent) of the unofficial imports consists of gold and/or Bangladesh currency to pay for Indian goods that are then smuggled into Bangladesh. The borders between India and Nepal are also porous. According to one esti-

Table 6-4. Key Commodities Traded in the South Asia Subregion, 1996, 1997, 1998
(thousands of U.S. dollars)

	1996		1997		1998	
Commodities	*Percent*	*Commodities*	*Percent*	*Commodities*	*Percent*	

India export to Bangladesh

Commodities (1996)	Percent	Commodities (1997)	Percent	Commodities (1998)	Percent
Total trade	100.0	Total trade	100.0	Total trade	100.0
Textile yarn	31.4	Textile yarn	27.3	Textile yarn	27.3
Cotton fabrics, woven	7.2	Rice	12.3	Rice	12.3
Rice	4.7	Cotton fabrics, woven	7.7	Cotton fabrics, woven	7.7
Motor vehicle parts and accessories	4.6	Lime, cement, building products	4.7	Lime, cement, building products	4.7
Iron, steel, plate, sheet	3.4	Iron, steel, plate, sheet	2.8	Iron, steel, plate, sheet	2.8
Lime, cement, building products	3.3	Coal, lignite, and peat	2.4	Coal, lignite, and peat	2.4
Stone, sand, and gravel	2.7	Motor vehicle parts and accessories	2.1	Motor vehicle parts and accessories	2.1
Cycles, etc., motorized or not	2.5	Rubber tyres, tubes, etc.	2.0	Rubber tyres, tubes, etc	2.0
Rubber tyres, tubes, etc.	2.2	Textile, leather machinery	2.0	Textile, leather machinery	2.0
Aluminium	2.0	Feeding stuff for animals	1.9	Feeding stuff for animals	1.9

Bangladesh export to India

Commodities (1996)	Percent	Commodities (1997)	Percent	Commodities (1998)	Percent
Total trade	100.0	Total trade	100.0	Total trade	100.0
Fertilizers, manufactured	92.0	Fertilizers, manufactured	92.7	Inorganic elements, oxides, etc.	44.0
Articles of plastic	7.1	Petroleum products	3.8	Fertilizers, manufactured	38.2
Tea	0.2	Tea	1.2	Tea	5.6
Alcohols, phenols, etc.	0.1	Alcohols, phenols, etc.	0.9	Iron, steel, plate, sheet	2.7
Fish, fresh, chilled, frozen	0.1	Metal tanks, boxes, etc.	0.5	Leather	1.7
Other machinery for special industry	0.1	Leather	0.2	Metal tanks, boxes, etc.	1.6
Under garments not knit	0.1	Textile articles	0.2	Mens outerwear not knit	1.2
Leather	0.1	Articles of plastic	0.1	Under garments not knit	0.8
Metal tanks, boxes, etc.	0.0	Special transactions	0.1	Petroleum products	0.8
Petroleum products	0.0	Floor coverings, etc.	0.0	Womens outerwear nonknit	0.5

Source: UN COMTRADE data, 1998.

mate, informal trade during the late 1970s and 1980s could have been eight to ten times more than the officially recorded trade.

In the late 1980s and early 1990s, all of the countries in the subregion began to lower their protective trade barriers and adopt policy reforms that have made these economies more open to the rest of the world and to each other. The South Asian Association for Regional Cooperation— India, Pakistan, Bangladesh, Sri Lanka, Maldives, Nepal, and Bhutan— was established in 1985. It began with the SAARC Preferential Trading Arrangement (SAPTA) and is currently pursuing measures to establish the South Asian Free Trade Area (SAFTA).

The push toward regional cooperation in South Asia is occurring in the context of important macroeconomic changes in these countries— growing liberalization, deregulation of industries and markets, reduction in the role of the state, and an expanding role for the private sector. While these processes are still nascent, there has been a steady increase in trade as a percentage of GDP (figure 6-3) and a growing economic dynamism that is reflected in robust income growth in the past decade, second only to that of East Asia (World Bank, 2000b). The share of trade to GDP for South Asia was 25 percent in the 1990-94 period. Export per-

Figure 6-3. Total Trade as a Percentage of GDP, Selected Regions

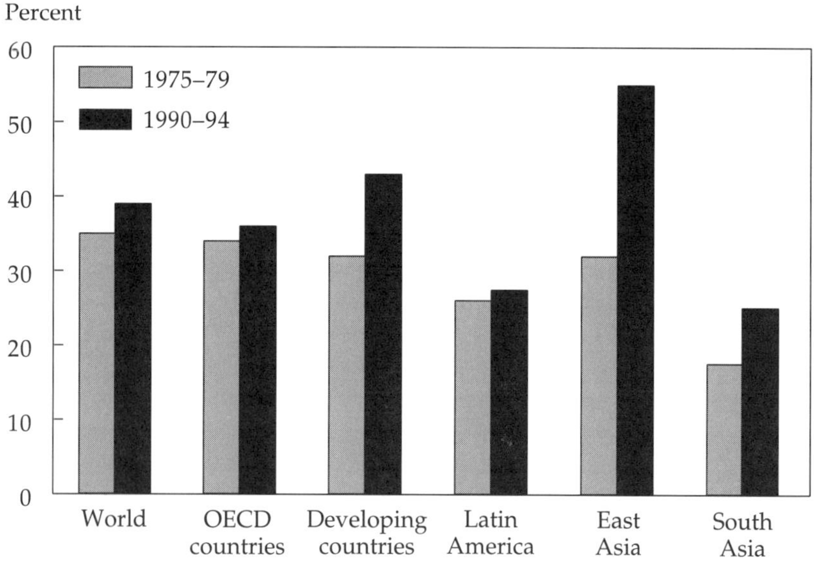

Percent

Source: Bandara and McGillivray (1998).

Figure 6-4. Real Export Growth in Bangladesh, India, and Nepal

Percent

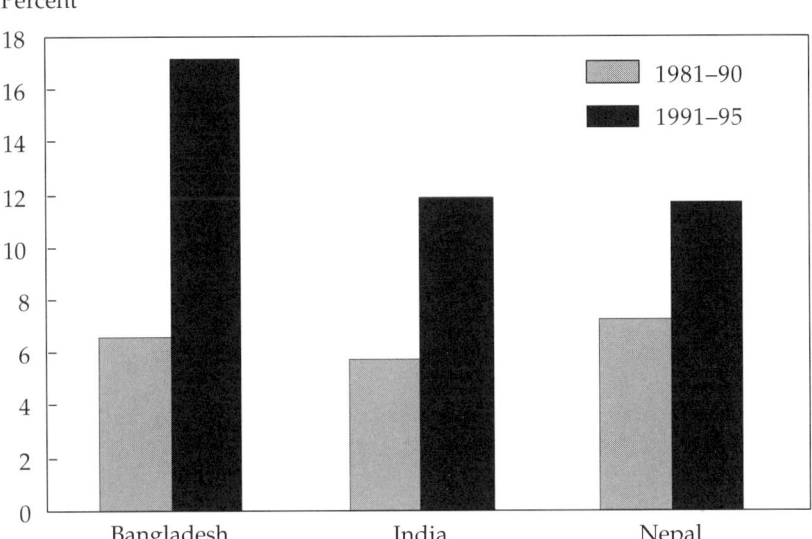

Source: Bandara and McGillivray (1998).

formance following trade reforms showed much improvement; Bangladesh's export growth is particularly impressive (figure 6-4). The share of manufactured exports as a proportion of total goods exports also grew rapidly.

Though intraregional trade is only a fraction of total trade and the growth rate of intraregional trade as percentage of total trade has been slow, in terms of absolute value there has been a multifold increase in intraregional trade. Between 1988 and 1998, India's exports to Bangladesh increased in value terms more than sixfold, while exports from Bangladesh to India multiplied four to five times. A similar pattern emerges for Nepal–India trade. Trade between Bangladesh and Nepal and between Bangladesh and Bhutan also rose, though not as steeply.

Transportation and Logistics Arrangements in the Subregion

With economic liberalization, private sector dynamism in South Asia is also rising. Domestic as well as international business communities are actively pursuing improvements in investments and trade in the region. A fundamental requirement clearly recognized and expressed by the

private sector is the need for streamlined transportation, trade facilitation, and logistics systems that would enable seamless movement of
goods and services within the region and to export markets in Europe
and the United States that demand high-quality products and "just in
time" deliveries. However, transport and logistics impediments continue
to constrain economic activities in South Asia.

The key transport and logistics impediments in the subregion are discussed below using data from selected sample commodity flows that
were examined in detail for a transport logistics cost study by the World
Bank (Subramanian and Arnold, forthcoming).[4] The analytic framework
applied in the evaluation of commodity movements on existing and proposed transit routes considered data on both the cost and time associated with the entire logistics chain, including the time and cost for
cross-border procedures and moving cargo through seaports.[5]

Excessive delays occur in moving cargo through the ports of Calcutta
and Chittagong for international trade.[6] Port congestion has led to inefficient handling of the cargo. Contributing to the delays are cumbersome customs procedures. Vessels cannot operate on a fixed day-of-the-
week schedule because of the uncertainty regarding the turnaround time
in the port. This adds to the time for ocean shipment of containers because the movement of the feeder vessels cannot be coordinated with
that of the mother vessels. Containers must wait in Singapore for up to a
week on average (Subramanian and Arnold, forthcoming).

Land border crossings also involve time delays and logistics costs that
are significant. Inefficient customs operations cause unnecessary queuing delays for inspection and customs clearance. Moreover, facilities are
inadequate for transfer of cargo between vehicles and for storage of cargoes that are being consolidated at the border. Poor physical planning
and uncoordinated operations cause serious congestion at the busier

---

4. The strategic commodities and routes selected for this study provide opportunities
for landlocked areas to reach local and regional markets or are critical commodities that
link the subregion to the global market.

5. The logistics cost model enabled two types of analyses. The first identifies the critical
impediments along a logistics chain—physical gaps and constraints, policies, procedures,
commodity type and market conditions—and then determines where efficiency improvements in the short term can bring about significant returns. The second type of analysis
compares existing routes with alternative routes (and modes) that have been proposed
by the private sector, are being considered by the concerned governments, or have potential for growth. The comparative analysis also allows a dynamic analysis of how improvements in the components of both logistics chains would affect overall benefits and
route selection.

6. Haldia port, India, was not included in the selected routes, although its role in handling the cargoes studied (tea, for example) is increasing rapidly.

crossings—for example, Petrapole (India) to Benapole (Bangladesh)—and lead to long delays at the less developed crossings where there is no customs office or customs official in residence (for example, the Banglabandh border in Bangladesh for Nepalese trade cargo).

Limitations on routes for transit cargo (regardless of which country owns the trucks) prevent shippers from taking the routes that offer the best balance of time and cost and from selecting the port that offers the least cost shipping to the overseas destination. This is true for regional movements also.

As in other regional trading blocs, in the South Asia subregion the bilateral protocol and transport/transit arrangements reflect low levels of mutual trust and confidence. For instance, no foreign vehicle is allowed on Bangladeshi roads. As a result all commodities transported by road to Bangladesh from the neighboring countries are transshipped at the border (transferred to Bangladeshi trucks). This greatly adds to the congestion, delays, and transportation costs at the border crossings. Nepalese trucks are allowed access only on dedicated routes within India; Indian trucks are allowed to enter Nepal and must depart within 72 hours.

Commodities to the northeastern Indian states from the rest of India still get routed around Bangladesh through the narrow land corridor mentioned earlier (the "chicken's neck"). The transportation cost and, in particular, time could be reduced significantly if the subregion would allow transit access for in-bond movement of Indian trucks through a dedicated corridor through Bangladesh.[7] In this case there would be no transfer of cargo from Indian to Bangladeshi trucks at the border crossings.

Table 6-5 compares costs and time for transportation of representative freight of all kinds (FAK) via two routes: the current route (via the "chicken's neck") and a potential transit route via Bangladesh by road. The latter route reduces the costs of transportation by 25 percent and cuts travel time by almost 50 percent. Transportation by railway and inland waterways offers similar savings for high bulk cargo. There is no bilateral agreement as yet between Bangladesh and India to move container traffic. By one estimate, it takes 45 days to move a container from Delhi to Dhaka: the container is moved via Tughlakabad to Mumbai and then shipped to Singapore, where it is brought by feeder ships to Chittagong port and then to the Dhaka inland container depot (ICD) by rail. The 2,000 kilometers between Dhaka and Delhi could be covered in

---

7. Countries in Europe and Central Asia allow free access for transit traffic from neighboring countries.

Table 6-5. The Cost and Time of Exporting Freight of all Kinds from Calcutta to Agartala, India, by Two Routes

Indicator	All India route[a]		Route through Bangladesh[b]	
	Cost (U.S. dollars)	Time (hours)	Cost (U.S. dollars)	Time (hours)
Transport and handling				
Inland transport	760	180	263	41
Cargo handling	278	18	270	20
Cross-border processing				
Cargo transfer	—	—	0	0
Customs inspection	—	—	75	12
Trade-related logistics				
Time cost of goods	73		96	
Insurance or pilferage and damage	240		180	
Documentation and forwarding	60		240	
Bank processing for Letter of Credit	96		96	
Key results				
Transport logistics cost	1,507		1,220	
Transport logistics time		198		73

— Not applicable.

Note: The shipment value is $24,000 and the shipment size is 8 tons.

a. The route is Calcutta-Raiganj-Siliguri-Gauhati-Karimganj-Agartala.

b. The route is Calcutta-Petrapole-Benapole-Daulatdia Ghat-Aricha Ferry-Narayanganj-Bhairab Ferry-Brahmanbaria-Ashuganj-Akhoura-Agartala.

Source: Subramanian and Arnold (2001).

two to three days according to estimates from the railways, but a bilateral protocol between the two countries would be needed.

Transport Infrastructure

Roads. Road transport is the principal mode for freight movements in the subregion. Medium-size trucks (a payload of 7 to 10 tons) operate on two-lane asphalt roads at relatively low average speeds (200 to 400 kilometers per day). The roads poorly maintained and congested in many parts. Only recently has India begun to upgrade its four major intercity roads to dual carriage ways. The movement of containers on the Indian roadways is limited not only by the design and condition of the roads and traffic congestion but also by nonphysical barriers to moving containers out of the port.[8] In Bangladesh the weight limits on the bridges between Chittagong and Dhaka, the main corridor for containerized goods, prevent the use of tractor-trailers.

India's load limit for trucks is 10 tons per axle. Bhutan and Nepal have similar limits. Bangladesh currently applies a limit of 8.2 tons, but this is expected to increase to 10 tons. Trucking services in all four countries are provided almost entirely by small private-sector owners and operators. Strong competition produces relatively low freight rates. These rates and the lack of strict inspection standards discourage the use of new trucks. The size of vehicles is limited by the capacity of the bridges, many of which are old, narrow, and in need of strengthening. The limits on total gross vehicle weight vary among the countries, but they are below the level required for efficient operation of larger trucks and tractor-trailers. The combination of weight limits and road conditions makes it expensive to move bulk commodities long distances by road unless the trucks are overloaded. Most of the trucks used in cross-border movements are two- to three-axle (six- or ten-wheel) trucks carrying payloads up to 18 tons. Trucks carrying bulk cargoes are generally overloaded, causing damage to poorly maintained roads.

Despite the differences in road dimensions and national limits on gross vehicle weight, there are no physical hindrances on the movement of trucks between the countries. Any constraints on cross-border movements are caused by insufficient capacity on the roads approaching the border, inadequate waiting area and customs checkpoints, and the lack of effective transit protocols. For example, Bangladesh does not allow trucks from other countries to travel on its roads. India reciprocates but does allow trucks from Nepal and Bhutan to operate on designated transit routes. Indian trucks are allowed into Nepal and are given a limit of 72 hours to carry cargo and return to India.

Railways. For a number of commodity routes, such as bulk cargoes between India and Bangladesh and transit cargo from Nepal, rail has a competitive advantage. The rail networks in India and Bangladesh are a mix of broad and meter gauge (Subramanian and Arnold, forthcoming, table 2.2). In India about one-third of the system is double tracked, and the Indian railways is making concerted efforts to convert its network to broad gauge in the Eastern region. The network is mainly meter gauge in eastern Bangladesh and predominantly broad gauge in the western

---

8. These containers adhere to standards set by the International Organization for Standardization, which is based in Switzerland.

part of the country, but the construction of the dual gauge rail link across the Jamuna Bridge, the extension of dual-gauge operations to Dhaka, and the planned introduction of dual-gauge track between Chittagong, Akhaura, and Tongi will substantially improve the coverage of the broad-gauge system. These developments could also provide a direct link between Chittagong and Nepal, as well as eastern India. Several other harmonization measures as well as additional border-crossings are under way or are being planned that will provide additional linkages between the western and eastern parts of Bangladesh and across the subregion.

There is a protocol for the interchange of rail wagons across the India-Bangladesh border that sets out the charges for the exchange of wagons and establishes a target wagon balance. Rail track does not appear to create a physical constraint for the movement of trains across the border, but Indian and Bangladeshi wagons have different coupling and braking systems that restrict operating speeds for Indian trains hauling Bangladeshi cars. Freight trains in India are typically 40 wagons in length compared with 35 wagons in Bangladesh. This means that Indian trains must be broken into two sections; the second section must wait for up to a week for another locomotive.

The constraints on regional freight movement by rail have less to do with technical physical constraints than with inefficiencies of the railway systems, which have lowered their share of freight traffic in the past few decades even within the countries. Both Indian and Bangladesh railways are publicly operated. Despite recent efforts to improve performance, they continue to suffer from overstaffing, poor maintenance, and old rolling stock. Bangladesh Railways also suffers from poor utilization of equipment. In India the movement of containers by railroad has increased substantially following the formation of Container Corporation of India and the procurement of a large fleet of cars for transporting standardized boxes. In Bangladesh the transport of containers is limited by the lack of cars and the operating commitment of the railroad. There are some block train movements between Chittagong and the Dhaka ICD, but these account for a very small portion of the containers handled at Chittagong (Parkash, 2000). Problems with rail services, charges, and port regulations limit the boxes that can be moved between the port of Chittagong and the Dhaka ICD to about 15 percent of the total volume moved through Chittagong.

Inland Water Transport. Inland waterways provide a potential lower cost alternative for low value bulk cargo by truck in the subregion. Bangladesh and India signed an Inland Water Transport transit protocol in 1980. The protocol allowed Indian barges to transit Bangladesh between West Bengal and Northeast India, but it prohibited transshipment of Bangladeshi cargo en route. In October 1999 a revised protocol was introduced that allows Indian barges to transport cargo between the two countries, provided that both countries share the transportation of cross-border trade and transit cargo on an equal tonnage basis.

Despite low costs and the absence of cross-border transshipment requirements, inland waterway transport is at a competitive disadvantage because of its low travel speeds (which average less than 50 kilometers per day due to the limitations on night navigation) and physical constraints on routes. Inefficiencies at border crossings in the subregion are attributable not only to protocol requirements, such as the one requiring transshipment at the border. Two other factors exacerbate the problem: (1) documentation and procedural inefficiencies for customs clearances and (2) physical infrastructure constraints (poorly designed warehouses, narrow access roads, and so on) that do not support efficient utilization of existing capacity.

Cross-Border Procedures

The existing procedures in the subregion are both cumbersome and time consuming, and they reflect the conservative trade policies that have characterized the region for decades. Customs clearance procedures can add significant costs and delays even though they represent a relatively small part of the logistics chain. Poorly defined or complex procedures and documents reduce transparency, especially when the approval of many people is required. Consider the key border crossing point Benapole (Bangladesh) to Petrapole (India) through which more than 80 percent of trade gets routed. Severe congestion results in long queues of trucks on both sides of the border (as many as 1,500 trucks) and waiting times of one to five days. As seen in table 6-6, yarn imports from Calcutta to Dhaka require an average travel time of about 270 hours. More than 85 percent of the time is spent at the border crossing on queuing, customs clearance, and transferring cargo to Bangladeshi vehicles.

Many of the documents submitted to customs at the border crossings in the subregion are similar to those commonly required at other international borders (such as invoices, packing lists, certificates of origin, letters of credit, and quarantine forms for plants and foods), while others are less common and specific to local requirements (such as import licenses, export permits, and various certificates). Since simplified procedures for in-bond movements and modern regulations for the carriage of goods have yet to be developed, equipment interchange certificates for containers and railway cars are needed and registration forms for vehicles and drivers moving across the border. The more fundamental

**Table 6-6. The Cost and Time of Importing Yarn by Truck
from Calcutta, India, to Dhaka, Bangladesh**

Indicator	Cost (U.S. dollars)	Time (hours)
Transport and handling		
Inland transport	516.00	17
Cargo handling	525.00	24
Cross-border processing		
Cargo transfer	80.00	156
Customs inspection	97.00	73
Trade-related logistics		
Time cost of goods	158.26	
Insurance or pilferage and damage	380.00	
Documentation and forwarding	285.00	
Bank processing for Letter of Credit	152.00	
Key results		
Transport logistics cost	2,193.26	
Transport logistics time		270

Note: The shipment value is $38,000 at Benapole (landing port).
Source: Subramanian and Arnold (2001).

problem is that the basic customs documents, such as transit, export,
and import declarations, vary from country to country and must be prepared separately for each side of the border and submitted in multiple
copies, with several signatures required. A standardized format would
not only reduce the paperwork but also encourage more consistent procedures and greater coordination between customs officials on either
side of the border. Although the requirements for the Nepal–India movements have been reduced in the past few years, considerable improvements are still needed.

Ports

Ports in the subregion pose a major constraint to international trade,
affecting both national and regional economies. Exporters from South
Asia cannot guarantee "just in time" deliveries in the global market. A
country's competitive position in the global markets is affected by its
reliability in delivery time and cost. The value of the cargo per unit volume or weight, its susceptibility to damage from handling, and physical
perishability and commercial shelf life greatly influence delivery time
and cost. Commodities that are either physically perishable (for example,

fruit, flowers) or have a short commercial shelf life (for instance, garments because of changes in fashions or trends) limit the feasible delivery time.

Transport logistics impediments en route, particularly at ports, adversely affect delivery time and costs. Carpet exports from Kathmandu to Germany, for instance, take almost 50 days to reach a European port (table 6-7). Similarly, the average time to move "time sensitive" ready-made garments from Dhaka, Bangladesh, to Los Angeles is about 35 days (table 6-8). Exports of ready-made garments are highly market sensitive in terms of cost and time because they have a short commercial life and are vulnerable to damage or loss. Carpets, on the other hand, have longer "shelf" life and are slightly less sensitive to damage but quite susceptible to loss. Since they are high-value commodities, however, they tie up capital when there are long delays in reaching final market.

As seen in the case of carpet exports from Nepal and garment exports from Bangladesh, the delays at Calcutta and Chittagong ports play a predominant role. Congestion within the ports, leading to inefficient handling of cargo, and cumbersome customs procedures add to the

Table 6-7. The Cost and Time of Transporting Carpets by Truck-Liner Vessel from Kathmandu, Nepal, to Bremen Port, Germany

Indicator	Cost (U.S. dollars)	Time (hours)
Transport and handling		
Inland transport	480.00	117
Cargo handling	260.00	74
Ocean freight	1,200.00	528
Cross-border processing		
Cargo transfer	261.00	164
Customs inspection	405.00	20
Trade-related logistics		
Time cost of goods	1,252.00	
Insurance or pilferage and damage	675.00	
Documentation and forwarding	450.00	
Bank processing for Letter of Credit	360.00	
Key results		
Transport logistics cost	5,343.00	
Transport logistics time		903

Note: The shipment value is $90,000 and the shipment size is one 20-foot equivalent unit.

Source: Subramanian and Arnold (2001).

Table 6-8. The Cost and Time of Transporting Cotton Garments by Truck-Liner Vessel from Dhaka, Bangladesh, to Los Angeles

Indicator	Cost (U.S. dollars)	Time (hours)
Transport and handling		
Inland transport	130.00	24
Cargo handling	311.00	28
Ocean freight	1,262.00	564
Cross-border processing		
Cargo transfer	33.90	170
Customs inspection	95.00	36
Trade-related logistics		
Time cost of goods	608.00	
Insurance or pilferage and damage	480.00	
Documentation and forwarding	120.00	
Bank processing for Letter of Credit	192.00	
Key results		
Transport logistics cost	3,231.00	
Transport logistics time		822

Note: The shipment value is $48,000 and the shipment size is 1 20-foot equivalent unit.
Source: Subramanian and Arnold (2001).

delays of waiting for feeder vessels that cannot operate on a fixed day-of-the-week schedule because of uncertainty in turn-around time at the ports. Containers from Calcutta and Chittagong are transshipped via Singapore or Colombo. Feeder services are provided by independent operators that transport boxes for several large container lines. The time required for the feeder movement and transshipment is about eight days—three days of sailing time and five days in the transshipment port waiting for the mother vessel.

For large shipments of neo-bulk cargoes, the cost of ocean transport is dependent on the size of the vessel. This is determined by the depth of the port as well as the size of typical consignments. The draft limitations at Calcutta, Haldia, Chittagong, and Mongla are 7.5, 8.4, 9, and 4 (7.5 at anchorage) meters, respectively. The routing of neo-bulk cargoes is generally determined by the availability of railroad and inland water access to the port having adequate depth. The protocols for handling transit cargo from other countries appear to be well established for these ports. The principal barriers to efficient transfer are the slow handling rates, restrictive labor practices, poor operational controls, and cumbersome customs procedures.

Bangladesh is currently implementing a preshipment inspection and valuation for selected imports at their port of origin in order to reduce the time required for customs inspection. Although this should improve transparency and reduce informal payments, it will not significantly reduce the time required for customs clearance because many of the delays are associated with the preparation of customs documents and inspections.

Improving port performance would bring direct benefits not only for regional commodity movements but, more importantly, for national economic development. The critical importance of an efficient gateway port for Bangladesh is obvious. The performances of Calcutta and Haldia ports have strong implications for the revitalization of Calcutta and West Bengal. More efficient ports, such as the Jawaharlal Nehru Port Trust (JNPT) at Nhava Sheva on the western coast of India, may offer a more cost-effective option for traders from eastern India and Nepal or Bhutan to reach European markets. The time and cost savings obtained at the port itself as well as during the ocean haul may compensate more than adequately for the longer distance the exporters would need to carry cargo to reach the port.

Table 6-9 compares the current route for Nepalese carpet exports (via Calcutta port to Germany) and a potential route through JNPT. The JNPT route indicates a 14 percent savings in transport costs and a reduction in travel time from nearly 38 days to 26 days (Subramanian and Arnold, 2001). A significant part of the time savings comes from the fact that Calcutta, unlike the JNPT, is a feeder port. Shipments from Calcutta are first taken to Singapore port and then loaded on to the international shipping lines to Europe after an average wait of 5 to 7 days at Singapore, whereas international shipping lines directly serve JNPT. However, the higher level of efficiency at JNPT (an average wait of 1.5 days compared with the 6-day wait at Calcutta port) should be noted.

More problematic than the total transport logistics time is the uncertainty of the actual time of the shipments due to the unreliability of the system. As interest in minimizing inventories and shortening reorder times has increased, so has concern for the reliability of shipment time and cost. Each link in a logistics chain poses a risk of additional delay and additional informal payments. Unfortunately, information on this variation is difficult to collect. Shippers' estimates in the subregion indicate that transport logistics costs could increase by 10 to 12 percent and logistics time by 40 to 60 percent for a significant percentage of consignments over the period of a year because of delays at the following points in the logistics chain:

- **Claiming shipment at the gateway port.** A bottleneck here can occur because of late notification that the ship has arrived, long prepa-

Table 6-9. The Cost and Time of Exporting Carpet from Kathmandu, Nepal, to Bremen, Germany, by Two Routes

	Traditional route[a]		Alternative route[b]	
Indicator	Cost (U.S. dollars)	Time (hours)	Cost (U.S. dollars)	Time (hours)
Transport and handling				
Inland transport	480.00	117	740.00	88
Cargo handling	260.00	74	463.00	155
Ocean freight	1,200.00	528	750.00	336
Cross-border processing				
Cargo transfer	261.00	164	125.00	37
Customs inspection	405.00	20	202.00	7
Trade-related logistics				
Time cost of goods	1,252.00		864.00	
Insurance or pilferage and damage	675.00		675.00	
Documentation and forwarding	450.00		450.00	
Bank processing for L/C	360.00		360.00	
Key results				
Transport logistics cost	5,343		4,629	
Transport logistics time		903		623

a. The route is Kathmandu-Birgunj/Raxaul-Calcutta Port-Bremen.
b. The route is Kathmandu-Bhairawa-Nautanwa-Moradabad-Mumbai (JNPT)-Bremen.
Source: Subramanian and Arnold (2001).

ration time for assembling documents for customs clearance, or other reasons. Port clearance time can increase by an average of 14 days.

- **Port terminal processing**. Equipment breakdowns can increase processing time by three days, and a port labor strike can cause delays of more than a week.
- **Customs clearance at the port.** Incorrect documentation, a broken seal necessitating a container inspection, or uncertainty over the dutiable amount of the import item, can increase the clearance time by one day to more than a week.
- **Egress from and access to the port.** Frequent political strikes and transport industry strikes outside the port cause congestion and inhibit mobility, thereby increasing the transit time by one day or several days.

- **Road-line haul between the port and the border crossing or destination.** Delays of one day to more than 15 days can result from truck accidents, truck breakdown, police inspection or harassment, the driver visiting home if it is along the route, truck bans in the city, ferry crossings, and other issues.
- **Land exit or entry port in the transit country.** Congested traffic access and egress, late arrival of sealed cover, and local political strikes can increase the processing time by one to several days.
- **Land entry or exit port in the destination country.** Incorrect or incomplete documentation, or disagreement over the description or classification of the goods as well as the valuation of the goods subject to customs duty, can increase the clearance time by two days to more than a week.

Conclusion

After evaluating the intraregional and international trade trends in the subregion, we suggest the following ways in which India, Bangladesh, Nepal, and Bhutan can achieve more efficient transport logistics.

Seaports are very important factors in determining route selection because of the long delays and high costs for transferring cargo through the ports. The elimination of unnecessary customs procedures and delays in cargo handling will cause cargo to be routed through more efficient seaports.

Customs clearances lead to unnecessary delays and informal payments. However, they do not have as great an impact on time and costs as other procedures at border crossings and ports. The uncertainties associated with the delays and costs of clearing customs can often be traced to inadequate preparation of customs documents by the shipper. Customs limitations on working hours, the low supply of officials at the border to clear consignments, the limited number of gates for receiving cargo, and the lack of transparency of procedures for inspection all reduce efficiency and create animosity. With simplified procedures, standardized documents, and limited inspections, especially for transit cargo, the congestion at the border could be substantially reduced or eliminated.

The constraints at land border crossings would be significantly reduced if protocols were established for unrestricted movement of cargo across borders in-bond. Instead, there is a provision preventing Indian, Nepalese, or Bhutanese trucks from moving across the Bangladesh border. India has reciprocal but restricted agreements with Bhutan and Nepal that allow trucks to move across the border. These constraints add to the cost of transport, not only because of the labor and losses involved in transferring cargo between vehicles but also because the shipper cannot choose the least-cost provider, and the transport companies cannot position themselves to obtain backhaul cargo other than at the border.

High-value exports from Nepal to the Pacific Rim require fast handling at Calcutta, Chittagong, and Haldia, whereas shipments to Europe and the East Coast of the United States require direct (intermodal) connections to the Jawaharlal Nehru Port Trust (JNPT). Both types of shipments require containerization of the cargoes at the earliest point in the logistics chain. The ability to ship in containers will be substantially improved with the operationalization of the three inland container depots on the Nepalese border. A direct rail link from Birgunj to the JNPT would provide the greatest efficiency gains among the alternatives considered.

Truck routes via Bangladesh can offer reductions in time and cost for medium-value goods moving between East India and Northeast India if the cargo can be moved in-bond, and there is coordination between customs checkpoints at border crossings on both sides of Bangladesh to significantly reduce delays and eliminate transshipment. The savings to the shippers should be sufficient to support tolls to cover the cost for road maintenance resulting from the increase in transit traffic.

For trade in high value goods between India and Bangladesh, trucks will continue to be the dominant, if not exclusive, mode. Travel time will be the major concern, and route selection will be based on reducing door-to-door delivery time. Significant improvements in rail operations would be needed if this mode were to capture some of this traffic. Trucking is provided almost entirely by the private sector, and it uses old vehicles with relatively low power-to-weight ratios, suitable for short-haul traffic but not for the long-haul movements of bulk and unitized cargoes. The rates for trucking services are competitive within the countries and between the countries, although India has the competitive advantage that it does not have to import trucks. The rates are held down by emphasizing low labor costs and inexpensive equipment rather than through efficient utilization of more expensive, higher capacity equipment. This is unlikely to change in the future until the road network is improved and until regulations regarding truck loads and safety are enforced.

Intraregional shipments of fruits, vegetables, and other perishable products from Bhutan and Nepal to India and Bangladesh require much better logistics. More emphasis is needed on reducing delivery time, increasing reliability of delivery, and minimizing losses en route to enable local manufacturers to compete for the supply of perishable products. Improvements can be achieved by allowing the cargo to move in a single truck from origin to destination and by ensuring that clearance time at the border on both sides does not require several hours.

The extension of the broad gauge network in India and the development of a dual gauge network in Bangladesh will broaden coverage and lessen delays. If the Indian and Bangladesh railways continue to integrate their systems and extend their broad gauge networks, then they might capture some medium-value cargoes. However, delays will continue at the border unless compatible rolling stock is introduced, and the shortage of locomotives ends. If these capital investments can be combined with more efficient operations as has been achieved by the Container Corporation of India, the railroads may be able to provide the quality of logistics services required by higher value goods. At a minimum, the railways will be able to hold their market share in their core business, the haulage of low-value bulk commodities, because of the higher costs for trucking and the longer transit times for inland water.

Inland waterways could play a more prominent role in the transport of the low-value bulk cargoes that move between Calcutta and North and East Bangladesh which is not yet served by broad gauge rail. The inland water transport network in Bangladesh is of considerable importance for domestic shipments but less relevant for the movement of transit traffic. Very low travel speeds could be compensated for by improvements in channel markings to allow for nighttime navigation and improvements in port operations to reduce turnaround time. However, this mode is expected to continue to attract only low value cargoes that can afford long delivery times. An exception is the proposed container on barge service between the proposed Patenga port and Dhaka that would take advantage of the poor rail container service and lack of efficient road connections for containers on this major corridor. Another exception is if the countries agree to Numaligarh refinery (Assam) products routed through Bangladesh to West Bengal.

Box 6-1 presents important recent efforts to improve transport logistics links in the subregion. As the countries more toward more open economies and expanded trade, both regional and international, in higher-value, finished goods, several critical issues still must be addressed. International markets are increasingly demanding tighter and more reliable deliveries. It is clear that without improved logistics, the subregion will not only miss out on new markets but will suffer a decline in market share in existing markets.

What improvements are most important? Six recommendations are offered in the remainder of the chapter. Some require action at the regional level; others, at the national level.

First, establish or amend bilateral transit protocols to allow for the movement of transit cargo across borders under bond without transshipment or inspection, reducing the constraints at land border cross-

Box 6-1. Recent Developments in Transportation in the Subregion

In the area of transport and trade facilitation, the following important developments clearly indicate the beginnings of change at the turn of the century:

- A "subregional quadrangle" consisting of Bangladesh, Bhutan, India, and Nepal was formed in 1998 under the South Asian Association for Regional Cooperation. Its purpose is to examine development opportunities in several sectors.
- "Champions" (people who have a stake in lobbying the government and authorities) have emerged to promote economic growth and development through improved investments, trade, and transportation in the subregion. In 1998 the Chambers of Commerce of Bangladesh, Bhutan, India, and Nepal signed a joint memorandum of understanding to this effect.
- India and Bangladesh renewed the Inland Waterways Transit Treaty in October 1999. This removed some of the anomalies that have existed for the past few decades, allowing for a more equitable transit opportunity that would benefit both countries.
- The Bangladesh and Indian governments launched a direct bus service between Dhaka and Calcutta in March 1999.
- Transshipment for Indian cargo through Bangladesh is being debated in Bangladesh. If well-conceived and regulated, this effort could benefit the eastern and northeastern parts of India and Bangladesh.
- India and Bangladesh railways are engaged in sustained efforts to integrate their railway systems. Both railways have completed the work for opening the Petrapole-Benapole border crossing in addition to the three existing crossings on the western side of Bangladesh. On the eastern side of Bangladesh, plans to connect rail links between Akhoura (Bangladesh) and Agartala (India) have already been agreed to by the two countries.
- The Phulbari treaty was signed in 1998 by the governments of Bangladesh, Nepal, and India. The treaty allows Nepalese goods access to Bangladesh markets through a dedicated transit route via India.

Pre-shipment inspection (for selected imports) was introduced in spring 2000 on a mandatory basis in Bangladesh.

Source: Subramanian and Arnold (2001).

ings. The new or amended protocols also should allow flexible routing for vehicles carrying transit cargo or imports through defined border crossings and replacement of the movement of transit cargo in trucks convoys to flexible movement against specified time limits.

Second, simplify and standardize the documents and clearance procedures required for cargo crossing land borders or exported or imported through the seaports. Reforms in this area would include the following:

- The use of secure seals for wagons or containers carrying transit cargo; few or no inspections of cargo at the border other than checking of the seals.
- Common vehicle inspection and licensing procedures for trucks used to transport cargo across borders.
- Automatic weighing of vehicles at border points.
- The Transports Internationaux Routiers (TIR) system for the carriage of goods approved by customs authorities.
- Simple procedures and risk assessment strategies to replace current cargo inspection practices.
- Round-the-clock clearance of cargoes at high-density interchange points like Petrapole-Benapole and Gede-Darsana.
- Development of full rake sidings, night unloading facilities, and terminal facilities at major loading and unloading points.
- Clearer assignment of liabilities. This permits tighter integration of intermodal movements and reduces barriers to entry for potential third-party logistic providers. It also makes railroads and trucking companies improve the quality of their service to limit their exposure from loss or damage of cargo.

Third, improve mechanisms for monitoring the movement of the cargo. To achieve this objective, countries should consider the following:

- Joint checking of cargoes at the origin and destination
- Electronic Data Interchange (EDI) between customs facilities within the country and across borders
- Identification numbers, bar codes, or other forms of electronic identification for trucks and cargo containers
- The use of a freight operation information system for real-time monitoring of trains, wagons, and cargo
- Tracking systems for transit cargo carried by trucks
- Implementation of a smart card system for expediting all the transactions associated with cross-border movements.

Fourth, expedite the transfer of responsibility for transport operations and services (but not necessarily infrastructure) from the public sector to the private sector. In addition, reduce the level of regulation of the providers of third-party logistics in a way that will encourage competition and allow for vertical integration of such services as transport, storage, consolidation, documentation, and clearance. Modern regulations should be introduced to govern the liabilities associated with the carriage of cargo by different modes. (See box 6-2 for private sector views.)

Box 6-2. Transport Logistics Improvements and the Private Sector

The private sector in Bangladesh, Bhutan, Nepal, and eastern and northeastern India is actively pursuing improvements in trade relations and transport logistics to ensure a smoother flow of goods and cost-effective services within the subregion. The Chambers of Commerce of the four countries have established a joint forum to examine and promote investment, trade, and the economic growth of the subregion. It is called the Emerging East Initiative. Participants from the subregion expressed strong dissatisfaction with the existing state of freight transportation to regional and international markets and the lack of consultation with users in bilateral and multilateral discussions on cross-country route and mode choices. In their view areas where the private sector could expand its role include operation and management of land-ports and logistics services facilities; the development of container transport, container operations, and facilities; cargo-handling facilities and services; freight-forwarding; customs clearance; financial services; storage and warehousing; and general transit and shipping services at sea ports and land border crossings. The private sector delegates' proposal for government action in trade facilitation included these recommendations:

- Harmonize government trade and transport policies and regulations in the subregion
- Amend transit treaties and protocols to allow for a freer choice of transport routes and service providers
- Institute a program of modernization for customs and cross-border facilities
- Increase the use of container transport by removing institutional impediments, such as the protocol between India and Bangladesh
- Construct ICDs in the region to encourage container transport outside of the main India rail transport corridors.
- Improve the access to credit and financial intermediation services in the region.

The actions recommended in this report build upon the general theme of consultation with the private and public sectors and would require action at the national and regional levels.

Source: World Bank (1999).

Fifth, invest in the transport network to improve the quality of logistics services. Investments, however, should be a lower priority than addressing procedural problems. The lower ranking is due in part to the recognition that these are long-term problems and will require major capital investment and increased private sector participation if they are to be solved.

Sixth, increase the use of containers for shipment of goods by developing ICDs that allow cargo to be stuffed and destuffed closer to the point of origin or the point of destination.

Finally, introduce electronic data interchange and business-to-business e-commerce to reduce logistics costs and time and overall transaction costs.

The changes that offer the largest benefits in terms of improved logistics are the revision of the current bilateral transit protocols, flexibility in transit cargo routing, and the increase in productivity at the seaports. Those offering significant benefits for both transit traffic and domestic traffic are improvements in the productivity of the railways and privatization of the transport services. The improvements in packaging, deregulation of logistics providers, and expansion of cyber trade offer the best long-term opportunities for reducing transaction costs and providing the quality of logistics required for high-value cargoes.

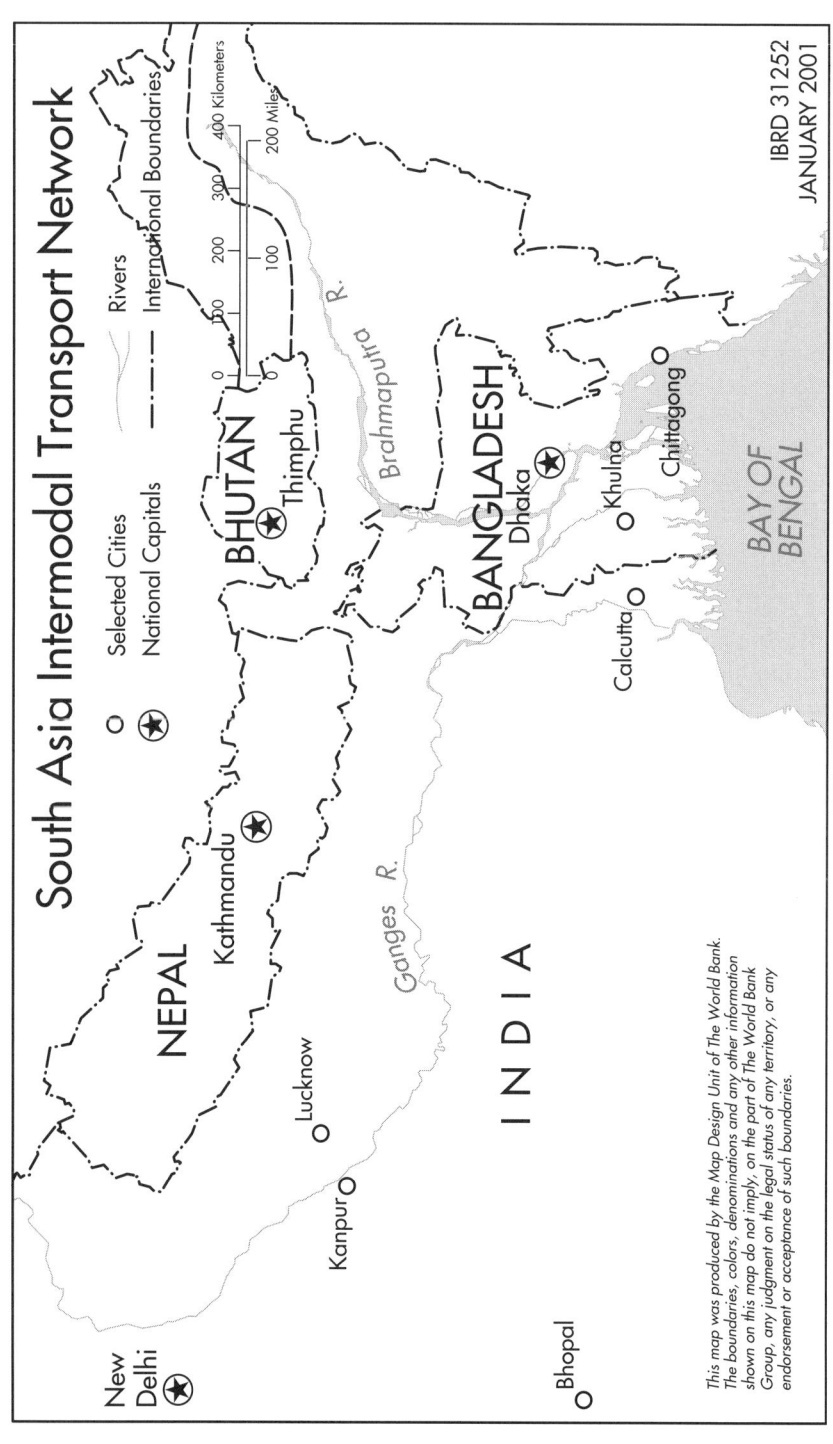

South Asia Intermodal Transport Network

Legend:
- ○ Selected Cities
- ⊛ National Capitals
- Rivers
- —··— International Boundaries

NEPAL

Kathmandu ⊛

BHUTAN

Thimphu ⊛

BANGLADESH

Dhaka ⊛

Brahmaputra R.

Ganges R.

I N D I A

New Delhi ⊛

○ Bhopal

Kanpur ○

Lucknow ○

Calcutta ○

Khulna ○

Chittagong ○

BAY OF BENGAL

0   100   200   300   400 Kilometers
0   100   200 Miles

IBRD 31252
JANUARY 2001

This map was produced by the Map Design Unit of The World Bank.
The boundaries, colors, denominations and any other information
shown on this map do not imply, on the part of The World Bank
Group, any judgment on the legal status of any territory, or any
endorsement or acceptance of such boundaries.

110

7

Urbanization and Regional Trade in South Asia: Issues and Options

Frannie A. Léautier

Economic growth in the past forty years has been closely associated with five phenomena: urbanization, industrialization, trade liberalization, technical change, and the emergence of new organizational forms. These arguments can be found in theoretical expositions, empirical evidence, as well as in the popular economic literature that drives conventional wisdom. For examples of such arguments see Aghion, Caroli, and Garcia-Penalosa (1999), Yergin and Stanislaw (1998), and World Bank (2000b).

The Asia region is undergoing high rates of urbanization and extremely high rates of industrialization, linked to increased international and regional trade. Unique organizational forms, such as the Grameen Bank in Bangladesh, co-exist with state and private sector organizations, playing an important role in the process of development. With respect to urbanization, urban growth rates of more than 3 percent per year are about at the same level as average global growth rates, but due to the high concentration of populations in urban areas, the absolute numbers of urban residents are orders of magnitude larger than in any other region of the world. By 2025, it is predicted that the region will have a majority of its people living in cities and towns (UNCHS Global Urban Observatory Database).

This transformation is phenomenal, particularly because an increasing number of poor will be living in urban areas. The size and urgency of the problem require different ways of managing cities and their related transportation and infrastructure requirements. There are very few sustainable cases of good management of the demand pressures for services in the cities of developing countries. Furthermore, macro and financial crises have cast doubt on well-held concepts and approaches. Countries that had achieved well-functioning cities with steady improvement over a period of twenty to thirty years have seen the collapse of city functions in the wake of the financial crises of the 1990s. Examples include Thailand, Indonesia, and Malaysia, which are now grappling with the emergence of the new urban poor. The increased pace of urbanization and its linkages to globalization have renewed interest in the process of urbanization and its links to economic growth. The major difference in the resurgence is the unit of analysis, which has shifted from nations to regions and from regional economies to the global economy. Cities have become the key point of entry for activities on the global scale.

Increased globalism has affected the functioning of cities and their hinterland economies in four important ways:

- Globalization of trade, with implications for the economic geography of city location
- Changes in demographics and income disparities in cities and countries
- Urbanization, densification, and city productivity
- Increased decentralization and awareness of governance.

Each of these shifts in the formation and functioning of urban centers will be discussed in turn.

Globalization of Trade and the Economic Geography of City Location

It has been observed that when you liberalize trade, you subject the country and its companies to external competition—fostering increased efficiencies and raising productivity. Well-functioning cities and their related infrastructure are critically important in companies' efforts to reduce costs and increase competitiveness. Therefore, there is a need to improve the performance of cities and their infrastructure in order to allow companies to remain in business locally, hence benefiting the local population, as well as to attract other companies to invest in one city over another.

Advances in international logistics have expanded the scope of international trade in goods and services. Global sourcing by manufacturing and service firms puts countries and cities in competition with each other. Comparative and competitive advantages are affected by transport endowment, policy, and performance. Cities can combine city governance and amenities with regional transport services to attract a variety of economic activities linked to global trade.

Nadiri and Mamuneas (1994) describe the link between company decisions to locate and city infrastructure services (such as road, rail, and air transport), as well as other services (such as water and electricity).

Anas and Lee (1988) and Anas, Lee, and Murray (1996) have focused on developing countries and the cost of doing business in them.

Transportation costs and access to immobile factors are key determinants of the comparative and competitive advantages of geography and location (Krugman, 1998). High transport costs can present barriers that result in little inter-regional trade, forcing the concentration of people in multiple urban centers of roughly equal size. According to Krugman, low transportation costs, on the other hand, tend to allow dispersion of economic activity to even-sized urban centers, or they can lead to concentration in megacities. Looking at patterns of urbanization in Asia, one can observe a co-existence of regions with high transportation costs and those with access to cheaper transport. The proliferation of small towns in countries such as Bhutan and Nepal, which are landlocked and hence dependent on their neighbors, is telling. Compare these small towns with the megacity phenomenon in Bangladesh, which stems from the challenges of climate and geography and their impact on the fluidity and interconnectedness of land transport systems.

How has this new globalism affected Asia, and what effect has it had, in particular, on the poorest subregion of Asia, which is composed of North East India, Nepal, Bhutan, and Bangladesh? In this chapter a survey of the trade patterns among contiguous countries in a subregion of Asia is used to assess the impact of increased trade among countries and its relation to city performance.

Trade patterns between countries in the region have changed dramatically, indicating regionalization in the midst of globalization. For example, export trade from Nepal to India doubled between 1996 and 1998 with a similar doubling of imports to Bangladesh from Nepal. Exports from India to its neighbors increased but to a smaller extent during the same period. Furthermore, huge trade imbalances between the countries exist (tables 7-1 and 7-2). For example, India exports fifteen times more than it imports from Bangladesh, and it exports two times more than it imports from Nepal. The impact of these imbalances on the demand for skills within each national economy and the implications for city growth and income disparities need to be investigated, but this issue is beyond the scope of this chapter.

Is an emergence of comparative and competitive forces among countries shaping these shifts? Infrastructure endowments, the main attractor of trade activity in the past, no longer seem to be sufficient to deliver development and comparative advantage, as can be seen when looking at the performance of infrastructure in the countries within this subregion.

When one compares the trade patterns to the conditions of road and rail infrastructure, one can see interesting patterns emerge. Nepal and Bhutan, the two landlocked countries with severe geographical challenges because of their location in the Himalayas, have roads in much

Table 7-1. Regional Pattern of Exports, 1996, 1997, 1998
(millions of U.S. dollars)

Export pattern	1996	1997	1998
India to Bangladesh	832	647	1,038
India to Nepal	158	147	324
Nepal to India	67	92	146
Nepal to Bangladesh	7	9	10
Bangladesh to India	21	37	55
Bangladesh to Nepal	0	1	18

Source: IMF (1999a, 1999b).

better condition than the roads in neighboring India and Bangladesh (table 7-3). The dedication to better road maintenance in Nepal and Bhutan may be driven by the pressure importers and exporters face because of high transport costs from transiting across large distances in these countries, which also do not have rail access inland (table 7-4).

Bangladesh, a country with severe climatic challenges, is abundantly served by ports and inland water transport systems. Therefore, transportation services can continue even with severe climate-related disruptions such as floods. The criticality of poorly performing roads and rail systems is reduced, since there are exit options for Bangladesh to use in terms of alternative modes of transport, as well as access to a world outside the region. One still needs to ask the question whether these transport mode options and access to an outside world have reduced the pressure to improve the efficiency of land transport systems that are critical for regional trade. A similar question can be posed of India, which has a large domestic economy that is relatively well protected and hence less subject to pressures to trade with others within the region.

Table 7-2. Regional Pattern of Imports, 1996, 1997, 1998
(millions of U.S. dollars)

Import pattern	1996	1997	1998
India from Bangladesh	58	39	65
India from Nepal	49	71	147
Nepal from Bangladesh	12	8	6
Nepal from India	442	436	440
Bangladesh from India	1,018	796	1,179
Bangladesh from Nepal	6	11	14

Source: IMF (1999a, 1999b).

Table 7-3. Road Infrastructure and Performance, 1988

Country	Density in kilometers per million persons	Condition (percent paved)
India	893	20
Bangladesh	59	15
Nepal	139	40
Bhutan	223	50

Source: World Bank (1994).

Other potential linkages between regional trade and the performance of cities and their related infrastructure are much more complex. It has been observed that more efficient regional transport systems, including in-land logistics services, as well as cities that afford better conditions for living because of superior management and investment, would enhance the chances that companies locate in one city and its subregion relative to another (Nadiri and Mamuneas, 1994). Such choices would, in turn, affect the demand for labor in the respective subregion as well as the income levels. However, not all company locations are expected to result in greater growth of a city. Aghion, Caroli, and Garcia-Penalosa (1999) show that it depends on the starting level of income of a city, the share of skilled labor relative to unskilled labor in the city, and the nature of the trade relations between a country and its neighbors. In particular, reduced transport costs and efficiencies from a well-functioning city in a country that exports primary products to a richer country would reduce the relative price of material inputs in the importing country, leading to further opportunities for growth for the importing country. It could also lead to changes in income disparities between skilled and unskilled labor: unskilled labor in the country exporting primary materials would gain a premium relative to skilled labor in that country and unskilled labor in the neighboring country, inducing reductions in in-

Table 7-4. Rail Infrastructure and Performance, 1988

Country	Rail traffic (kilometers per million $ GDP)	Diesels in use (percent of diesel inventory)
India	593	90
Bangladesh	41	73
Nepal	None	None
Bhutan	None	None

Source: World Bank (1994).

come disparities in the exporting country, while sharpening income disparities in the importing country, if both countries start off with the same ratio of skilled to unskilled labor.

Nepal and Bhutan have a lower incidence of poverty than Bangladesh. (See discussion later in chapter of table 7-9.) The trade relations between the countries coupled with the better functioning land transport in Nepal and Bhutan may be the key explanatory factors here.

Changes in Demographics and Income Disparities in Cities and Countries

Regional trade affects city growth and performance. Urbanization and industrialization, it also has been argued, result in an increase and then a decrease in income inequality. Simon Kuznets (1955) found an inverted U-shaped relation between income inequality and GNP per capita. This result was interpreted as describing the income inequality that arises as city residents begin to earn more than rural residents, when companies employ city residents at higher wages in industrial production. A reversal in this trend is expected once cities grow to the point that they attract more rural labor. Another argument relates to the increased demand for production of agricultural goods in cities. This contributes positively to growth in rural areas, thus reducing the disparity between urban and rural incomes and raising incomes overall.

Countries can be caught in a vicious cycle of urbanization, low economic growth, and rising income disparities. Stagnation in agriculture results in the inability of the rural sector to support higher demand in cities. Such countries would then import agricultural products to feed city residents, and income disparities would continue to grow (figure 7-1).

Many countries in Asia and Africa are facing high urbanization rates with little or no positive impact on growth. This appears to support the vicious-cycle hypothesis. To determine a way out of the quandary caused by urbanization, increased inequality, and low growth, these countries should examine both the performance of cities and the pattern of trade with other countries. It is rare to find an analysis of trade liberalization and/or privatization that is posited in the context of the competitiveness of cities in a country and what they have to offer to companies wishing to locate or invest there.

The varying patterns of regional demographics in Asian cities highlight the dilemma these cities face (table 7-5). Cities in Asia and the Pacific have more than double the city populations in other regions. Although the average pace of growth of Asian cities is about the same as the average growth rate of cities in developing countries, because of the

Figure 7-1. The Vicious Cycle of Urbanization, Low Economic Growth, and Rising Income Disparities

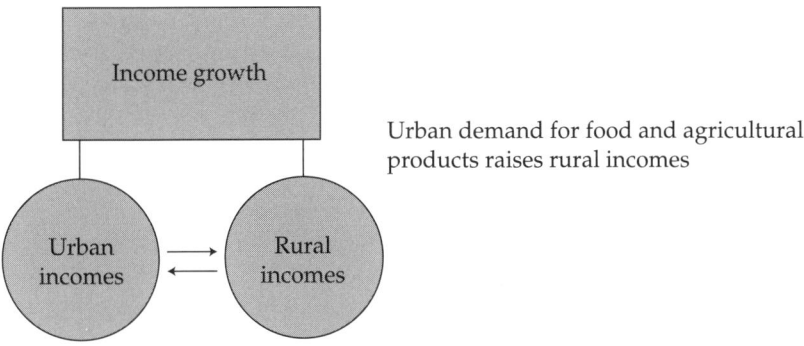

Urban demand for food and agricultural products raises rural incomes

Stagnation in agriculture or productivity growth in rural areas pushes people to cities. If cities cannot absorb them, urban poverty worsens.

Source: Author's construction using evidence from World Bank (2000a).

starting size of populations in Asian cities, the order of magnitude of change is more serious.

High concentrations of population, measured by persons per hectare, are another attribute of Asian cities, with average densities of 237 persons per hectare compared with 168 for typical cities in developing countries. A high concentration of residents in large cities should contribute to higher income growth, lower income disparities, and eventually higher productivity, with an expected reversal in the dynamics predicted by Kuznets (1955).

Table 7-5. Varying Patterns of Regional Demographics, 1993

Region	Average city population (in thousands)	Average growth per year (percent)	Average density (persons per hectare)
Asia and the Pacific	3,100	3.2	237
Developing countries	1,480	3.5	168
Worldwide	1,500	3.1	154

Source: UNCHS (1995b).

Table 7-6 compares the income disparities and city product (dollars per person) in Asia to other regions. Income disparities, measured by the ratio of the 20th highest income percentile to the 20th lowest income percentile, are much lower in Asian cities. The ratio of 6.7 for Asian cities is much lower than that of 10.7 for other cities in the world. Asia as a region has also grown at a very fast rate in the past twenty years, lending credence to the second phase of the Kuznets hypothesis. However, the productivity of Asian cities, measured by the city product per person of $1,059, is considerably lower than the average of cities in developing countries ($1,546), and the worldwide average ($4,411). This means that there is a lot of untapped potential for productivity in Asian cities that can be unleashed. The trick is to find the right approach to making cities much more productive.

Within-region demographics can shed light on the arguments posed so far. The similarity of average growth rates in Asian cities to the worldwide average growth rate of cities camouflages distinct patterns of growth within Asia. The growth rate of Asian cities varies widely depending on size and density as well as other factors. High rural-urban migration has fueled fast and uncontrolled urban growth in many Asian cities, which have attracted rural residents seeking employment because of the lack of opportunities in rural areas. Population concentration in increasingly large metropolitan areas is a phenomenon noted earlier. It highlights the growing importance of secondary cities and towns.

Table 7-7 demonstrates some of these trends, which can be characterized as centripetal and centrifugal forces driving city growth (Krugman, 1998). A city such as Lahore is characterized by medium density, high growth, and high city product relative to other cities in the region. Chittagong is characterized by medium density and fast growth but low city product. This suggests that these two cities attract residents in a dispersed manner, with low densification and more spatial spread than in other cities in the region. There are also opportunities for Lahore and Chittagong to improve their productivity. A look at the city transporta-

Table 7-6. Income Disparities and City Product, 1993

Region	Income disparity[a]	City product (dollars per person)
Asia and the Pacific	6.7	1,059
Developing countries	10.7	1,546
Worldwide	10.7	4,411

a. The ratio of the 20th highest income percentile to the 20th lowest income percentile.
Source: UNCHS (1995a).

Table 7-7. Centripetal and Centrifugal Forces in Urbanization Patterns in the South Asia Region, 1993

City	Population (in thousands)	Density (persons per hectare)	Growth rate (percent)	City product (dollars per person)
Mumbai	10,265	603	2.04	275
Chittagong	2,400	61	5.34	218
Bhiwandi	553	934	22.88	341
Lahore	4,509	37	3.59	428
Colombo	4,390	86	0.49	1,036

Source: UNCHS (1995b).

tion and services as well as congestion and air quality, which are well-known problems, may be necessary for these cities to improve their productivity. Issues related to the management of these cities may be critical as well.

Bhiwandi, with a density of close to 1,000 persons per hectare, is growing at close to 23 percent per year. The city product of Bhiwandi is much higher than that of Chittagong but lower than that of Lahore. What is happening in Bhiwandi to deliver this type of performance? The pressures of managing a city growing and densifying at such high rates as Bhiwandi, starting from a low base of 553,000 persons, are daunting. The skills needed in these cities to manage such high levels of growth are in short supply. Yet something about Bhiwandi is attracting business and residents.

What about Colombo with a city product that is much higher than any other city in table 7-7? What does Colombo do to deliver such high performance while remaining low density and relatively small. How has it avoided becoming a megacity? One answer may be the Sri Lankan government's investment in transport infrastructure in rural areas that connect to Colombo. The policies on urban density in Colombo and the implications for land markets may be another clue.

Bombay, with more than 10 million people, high density, and a growth rate above 2 percent per year, exemplifies the opposite complexity of managing megacities. Fast-growing small towns and continued growth and densification of megacities present very different management challenges as well as complex demands for transport and infrastructure. How do firms view these patterns of city development and performance? How do the management and investment decisions made by cities affect firms' decisions on where to locate?

Urbanization

Another unique phenomenon is the increasing concentration in large cities across all countries in the Asia region. There are 25 cities with a population of more than 1 million in the Asia region compared with 86 cities of that size worldwide (table 7-8). The distribution of cities by city size in Asia is telling. Asia is well known for its megacity phenomenon. Seventy-six percent of the cities in the region have a population above 300,000. Almost 60 percent are classified as megacities—that is with populations above 1 million, and growing. In short, urbanization in Asia, with its megacity phenomenon, is distinctly different from that of other regions.

Why does Asia have a larger concentration of megacities than all other regions of the world, including industrialized countries? Is it because of trade liberalization and industrialization à la Kuznets (1955), or because of transport costs and geography à la Krugman (1998)? The answer will influence the type of policies needed to tackle the challenges of poverty reduction facing these cities.

Urban poverty is growing faster than the rate of urban growth in South Asia (table 7-9). Population pressure, country size, and regional inequalities shape the pattern of development and define the role of transport in the region. Cities are beginning to function as "systems of cities." The quality of city management interacts with transport policy and performance to shape further urbanization.

Cities such as Colombo are able to achieve higher city product with low densification and low growth rates. What is the link to hinterland transport services and the regional economy that allows such productive outcomes? How differently do companies and municipal authorities need to serve Bombay compared with Colombo or Bhiwandi? What is the role of transport in such a pattern of regional and city growth and performance? These are all questions that can be addressed by looking at the other shifts mentioned earlier.

Table 7-8. Number of Cities by Size, 1993

	City population		
Region	Less than 300,000	300,000 to 1 million	More than 1 million
Asia and the Pacific	9	8	25
Industrial countries	8	13	13
Worldwide	77	66	86

Source: UNCHS (1995b).

Table 7-9. Demographic Characteristics of Selected Asian Countries

Country	Population (in millions) 1998	Area (in thousands of square kilometers)	Per capita GNP (in U.S. dollars)	Percentage of population below poverty line
India	980	3,288[a]	430	35.0
Bangladesh	126	144	350	35.6
Nepal	23	147	210	42.0
Bhutan	0.8	47	430	—

— Not available.
Note: These figures do not reflect official World Bank policy.
a. Including part of Kashmir.
Source: World Bank (2000b).

Decentralization and Governance

Decentralization of government also has an impact on city size. Countries that are decentralized politically and administratively tend to have more even-sized cities than do those that are centralized. It is argued that the concentration of political power in centralized countries leads to concentration of economic power in the capitals of those countries and/or states and hence to the phenomenon of megacity formation (Krugman, 1998).

Dhaka in Bangladesh stands outs as a dominant city, indicating a relatively low level of decentralization in Bangladesh, and Asia as a region has a predominance of megacities, indicating that the region overall may be more centralized politically than other regions of the world. Focusing on the degree of decentralization and transport costs in a globalizing world is important if cities are to tap into the potential of the global economy.

There are a number of forces at play that are driving the process of decentralization. In particular, the constrained fiscal environment at the central government level has driven decentralization in the Asia region and around the world. As national governments seek to rationalize their expenditures, they continually push for accountability at lower levels of government (Prud'homme, 1995).

Within the South Asia region, there is growing reliance on local bodies in service delivery, but these bodies have weak management capacity and do not have sustainable finances. The capacity of local governments to manage their cities affects the comparative advantage of cities. Well-managed cities attract business and residents since they are able to cater to the demand for services. The size and importance of local bodies shape the competitive position of cities as well as the quality of their management. Intercity and intracity transport is key to tapping the potential of these governance advantages.

Good Governance and Cities' Comparative Advantages

The Kathmandu-Biratnagar-Dhaka-Chittagong corridor is used to illustrate the connection between good governance and a city's comparative advantage in capturing regional trade and international investment. This corridor goes through four key cities, three of which are major cities in their countries: Kathmandu in Nepal and Dhaka and Chittagong in Bangladesh. The traffic in this corridor in 1998 was estimated at 420,000 tons per year, with a potential to double (Stevens and Cook, 1999). Options for transport in the corridor include transportation by road if using Chittagong port, or transportation by rail and road if using Calcutta. These options enable Chittagong and Calcutta to compete for regional trade outflows and inflows. The performance not only of the ports but also of the cities becomes critical. Chittagong may be as productive a port as Calcutta, but if Calcutta is a better managed city, it could attract business away from the port of Chittagong and vice versa. This case illustrates the interlinkages between the performance of transport services and city management.

Table 7-10 highlights other factors in this example. Kathmandu, with a population of 472,000, is growing at 5.8 percent per year. For effective growth in Kathmandu, the performance of Biratnagar, Dhaka, Tangail, and Chittagong is critical, as are good transportation links between these cities. Regional trade makes cities in one country dependent on the performance of cities in other countries with which they are linked by trade.

Table 7-10. City Performance, 1993

City	Population (in thousands)	Income disparity[a]	Annual growth rate (percent)	City product (dollars per person)
Kathmandu	472	—	5.8	—
Biratnagar	138	—	3.4	—
Dhaka	6,610	6.88	5.5	219
Tangail	158	6.88	3.4	172
Chittagong	2,400	6.88	5.3	261

— Not available.

a. The ratio of the 20th highest income percentile to the 20th lowest income percentile.
Source: UNCHS (1995b).

Measures of the Importance of Local Governments

The ability of a city to manage its responsibilities depends on the importance afforded to local governments. Three measures of the importance of local governments are examined: the size of the employee base, financial management and transparency, and the autonomy of cities in national economies.

Size of Employee Base

Dhaka has a sizable workforce at the city level, close to three times that of Kathmandu and Chittagong (table 7-11). This means that the local government in Dhaka has the potential to administer power at the city level. How this will positively affect Kathmandu depends on regional externalities beyond the management of Dhaka as a city. For Kathmandu to continue to grow, it may need to depend on Dhaka's performance; of course, Kathmandu does not have any influence on the governance or management of Dhaka, except potentially through trade and transport. The size of the employee base in Dhaka could be a hindrance to reforms if reforms, such as privatization of water services in the city, are difficult and resisted by the local government employees. Therefore, greater size does not always mean improved performance.

Financial Management and Transparency

In addition to measures of importance of a local government, defined by the size of its employee base, we can look at indicators of performance of a local government that are more direct, such as financial management and transparency.

Three readily accessible indicators of financial management and transparency are the revenue per capita, capital expenditures per capita, and

Table 7-11. Local Government Importance, 1993

City	Local government employees per 1,000 poopulation
Kathmandu	2.46
Biratnagar	1.58
Dhaka	6.15
Tangail	0.72
Chittagong	2.17

Source: UNCHS (1995b).

the percentage of works at the city level that is contracted out to the private sector. On all three indicators Dhaka ranks by far the highest (table 7-12). Dhaka spends per capita almost as much as it collects in the form of revenue per capita, and it relies more heavily than the other cities in the table on the private sector to carry out the works. This raises the question of the very large size of Dhaka's employee base and how it is deployed. Tangail spends a lot more per capita than it raises in revenues, indicating a high reliance on central government transfers and thus a potential for increasing its autonomy should it choose to do so. Chittagong and Kathmandu spend a lot less per capita than they collect in revenues, raising a number of questions as to what happens to the revenues. Such intercity comparisons in performance in a globalizing world will determine more and more the degree to which residents and businesses choose to locate in these cities.

Globalization will pressure cities to improve the level of services they provide to their residents, and it will also exert pressure on companies that choose to locate in these cities. We will begin to see more of the effects of this type of pressure as companies locate internationally on the basis of city performance rather than country performance and as regional economies become linked more closely.

Autonomy of Cities in National Economies

The autonomy of city governments is also a critical determinant of how residents and businesses view cities and the related demand for infrastructure and transport services. In Kathmandu, Biratnagar, Tangail, and Chittagong the central government can shut down local governments (table 7-13). Furthermore, with the exception of Tangail and Chittagong, the central government can remove all councillors in those cities. Other indicators of autonomy include the ability to set and charge taxes, the

Table 7-12. Financial Management and Transparency, 1993

City	Revenue per capita (1993 U. S. dollars)	Capital expenditure per capita (1993 U. S. dollars)	Percent contracted to the private sector
Kathmandu	8.4	3.82	
Biratnagar	5.5	1.98	45
Dhaka	27.7	25.33	74
Tangail	1.4	14.94	32
Chittagong	9.2	1.97	41

Source: UNCHS (1995b).

Table 7-13. The Power of the Central Government, 1993

	The central government can	
City	Close local government	Remove councillors
Kathmandu	Yes	Yes
Biratnagar	Yes	Yes
Tangail	Yes	No
Chittagong	Yes	No

Note: No data were available for Dhaka.
Source: UNCHS (1995b).

ability to borrow, and the ability to contract out (table 7-14). Cities in Bangladesh seem to have more autonomy to carry out these functions than those in Nepal.

Although Nepali cities have reduced autonomy, they may enjoy advantages in inter-regional networks of services. This illustrates the importance of balance between local autonomy and regional perspective in making determinations of service delivery to support higher growth.

Potential Challenges

The cities in South Asia face many challenges. Because of the constraints that go with managing a megacity, Dhaka may not be able to react in an agile and flexible manner to the demands of residents or companies wishing to conduct business there, and it may have difficulty instituting change because of the large size of its employee base. Dhaka can be overtaken by a city such as Tangail, which may prove to be more agile. Megacities in the region such as Mumbai need to pay attention to this phenomenon as it may pose a threat to their ability to attract certain

Table 7-14. The Power of the Local Government, 1993

	The local government can		
City	Set taxes and charges	Borrow	Contract
Kathmandu	Some	Some	All
Biratnagar	Some	Some	All
Tangail	All	All	All
Chittagong	All	All	All

Note: No data were available for Dhaka.
Source: UNCHS (1995b).

types of businesses, with implications for their ability to grow and to reduce income disparities.

Governance, as measured by transparency and autonomy, may give advantage to Tangail and Biratnagar over Dhaka and Kathmandu. All cities need to be aware that governance structures strongly influence whether they will have sustained capacity to grow and to reduce income inequalities. With the fickleness demonstrated by international capital markets, cities will increasingly become the stage on which international competition takes place.

Chittagong city may be performing well, but issues need to be resolved in Chittagong port to protect its position relative to Calcutta. Port cities have a special function in relation to each other. Most countries focus policy reforms on the port sector, and on liberalization of trade, rather than on, or in addition to, the performance of port cities.

Conclusions

How does a country incorporate these global trends into a strategy for regional development and trade that has cities and their management at center stage? Since cities can be very significant in leveraging the effect of globalization, it would be prudent to lay out the basic elements of such a strategy. It has four parts.

First, draw up holistic frameworks that sharpen strategic vision, recognizing the schizophrenic aspects of urban development that can simultaneously lead to economic growth and a reduction in income disparities. This would require forging coherence between the community desire for results at the city level, private sector interests in profits, and national interests in trade and competitiveness. Countries would need to develop and tolerate the co-existence of city-wide and region-specific solutions that could be vastly different.

Second, introduce long-term system-wide approaches rather than project approaches to investment in urban areas and regional transport, with a focus on development impact. This would allow countries to use their endowments in infrastructure and the wealth in human and physical capital resident in their cities, as well as their capacity to manage cities in a globalized world.

Third, learn from others and focus on long-term institutional building, understanding that change requires a process of transforming urban societies. National and regional institutions are also needed to unleash the potential of regions to attract economic activities.

Fourth, move toward regional rather than national programs, understanding spatial aspects and "systems of cities." Economic and geographical boundaries, rather than national boundaries, pose the greatest constraints in the twenty-first century.

8

Rotterdam:
A Strategic Hub in the
Global Trade-Transport Chain

T. R. Lakshmanan

Rotterdam became the largest port in the world in 1962. Since then it has maintained its premier rank in the global port system during a period of turbulent change: a shift worldwide from a material- and energy-intensive industrial structure to a knowledge-intensive industrial structure, globalization of manufacturing processes and organization of production and related services, relocation of industries across national borders and the emergence of global production networks, and major changes in transport and the complementary information technologies that support this worldwide production and trading system.

Such economic transformations in the scale, geographic location, and industrial mix of production imply vast and complex changes in the context and scope of the transportation function. The volume, composition, origin, and destination of cargo have changed, as well as the speed, price, reliability, and timeliness of movement—in other words, what moves, how it moves, and where it moves. Clearly, the maritime industry and port operations had to be restructured to function efficiently in this dynamic environment.

Rotterdam's continued dominance as a transport hub in the global transport system is a tribute to its ability to strategically position itself for growth in a changing economy. It exemplifies a major transport facility that assesses the broad economic and transport environment, plans ahead, and invests in physical technologies and infrastructures and in human and institutional capital that promote the port's adaptability for growth and leadership.

The aim of this chapter is to highlight the factors that underlie Rotterdam's success as a major hub in the world's trade-transport chain. Two distinct and related activities serve as a metaphor for the port's history of strategic alertness, flexible adaptation, and success: (1) the planning and provision of the best-practice trade-transport chain services for port users today, and (2) strategic redefinition of the port's future functions and investments that maintain growth in a dynamic context.

Specifically, the planning and provision of the state-of-the-art trade-transport chain services for port users are accomplished through timely investments in transportation and information infrastructures and in non-physical infrastructure (knowledge and competencies in transport and trade facilitation). The latter involves restructuring and reform of the following:

- Overall governance of transport and trade facilitation into, in, and from the port
- Logistical operations in the port
- Operational coordination of different port users, and
- State-of-the-art techniques for controlling physical flows in the port.

Rotterdam has made financial and organizational investments in the emerging markets (for example, the Czech Republic) in its hinterland, and it has developed innovative support services for the coordination of production and distribution activities of global corporations that are tenants of the port—thereby stimulating future growth.

This chapter reviews Rotterdam's history as a port that has built on its physical and locational resources, its commercial linkages to major European economic centers, and its timely investments in physical, human, and institutional capital. A statistical and comparative economic profile of Rotterdam is then presented. In the final section we offer a case study of a port that has reinvented itself as a major hub in the global economy by providing best-practice trade-transport chain services for port users and by redefining the port's function in the future.

From Fishing Port to European Mainport

The history of Rotterdam from its humble beginnings in 1328 as a fishing port on the River Rotte to its current position as Mainport Europe is remarkable. Rotterdam was a prosperous old Dutch port, its fortunes tied to the growth and the decline of the commercial hegemony of the Dutch Republic from 1500 to 1800. In the nineteenth century, with the industrialization of the United Kingdom and Germany, demand increased for transport of raw materials and finished goods. In 1864 Rotterdam started the construction of a navigation channel without locks directly to the sea (Nieuwe Waterweg), and it was selected as the import and export port for the German coal and steel industry. This marked the beginning of bulk transport in the port. During the decades leading up to the Second World War, investments in the form of deeper channels and tank storage and industrial land consolidated the port's position and enabled its emergence as a petrochemical production site.

The reconstruction of the port after wartime bombing provided a newer vintage of port capital stock, an expansion of petroleum operations, and the establishment of a large chemical industry and the world's biggest oil industry complex. As the European economy recovered from the war, Rotterdam port became in 1962 the biggest port in the world.

Since then the port has continued to offer state-of-art-services to its users by responding to major changes in the industry: it increased ship size—deepening Nieuwe Waterweg to 62 feet in 1969, with progressive increases to the current depth of 72 feet; it organized a container shipment company (ECT) and its facilities in reclaimed land at Maasvlakte; and it developed the port as a global distribution center.

Rotterdam: A Statistical and Economic Profile

Rotterdam has long been the busiest route for exporting and importing goods into Europe, given its deep harbor stretching 30 miles inland, its central location vis-à-vis the continent's 350 million consumers, its diverse facilities (multi-user, multimodal, and dedicated facilities that can handle sixth-generation vessels), and its progressive business spirit and know-how.

The connections that Rotterdam has developed to the important cities in its hinterland in terms of attractive time-distance and services add to its appeal to its far-flung customers. Door-to-door delivery from Rotterdam is available to most European destinations by efficient intermodal transport.

Goods are delivered from Rotterdam to most European markets within 48 hours. It offers nonstop shuttle trains to many cities, feedership service to 110 European ports, and scheduled barge service via a dense network of inland waterways to other cities. Table 8-1 illustrates the range of frequently scheduled intermodal connections from Rotterdam to close-in cities like Bramerhaven (Germany) or to distant places such as Lisbon, Istanbul, and St. Petersburg.

Rotterdam dominates the European port world, handling nearly three times as much tonnage as Antwerp, the next port (figure 8-1). As noted earlier, Rotterdam is also the world's largest port—well ahead of Asian ports like Singapore and Shanghai (figure 8-2), and it continued its growth in the 1990s.

The composition of Rotterdam's cargo is heavily weighted toward liquid bulk goods (petroleum), and dry bulk goods (ores, scrap, coal,

Table 8-1. Rotterdam's Multimodal Connections to Selected European Cities, 1998

City	Kilometers from Rotterdam	Road (time in days from Rotterdam/ frequency)	Rail (time in days from Rotterdam/ frequency per week)	Inland waterway (time in hours from Rotterdam/ frequency per week)	Short-sea feeder (frequency per week)
Copenhagen	797	1 / daily	1.5 / 5	n.a.	8
Prague	960	1 / daily	1.5 / 5	n.a.	n.a.
Bramerhaven	418	0.5 / daily	1.5 / 5	60 / 3	9
Milan	1,294	1.5 / daily	2 / 5	n.a.	n.a.
Basel	800	1 / daily	1 / 5	72 / 7	n.a.
Oslo	1,350	2 / daily	4 / 5	n.a.	11
St. Petersburg	2,720	3 / daily	13 / 5	n.a.	2
Lisbon	2,245	2.5 / daily	6 / 5	n.a.	9
Istanbul	3,000	3 / daily	10 / 2	n.a.	3

n.a. Not applicable.
Source: Port of Rotterdam (1998b).

Figure 8-1. Total Throughput in Main EU Ports, 1995–98

Millions of metric tons

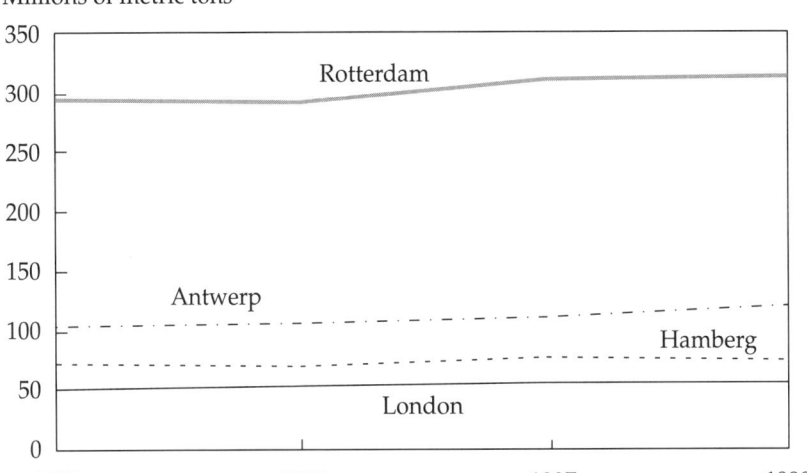

Source: Rotterdam Port Information Centre, February 2000.

agribulk) associated with the manufacturing sector of Mainland Europe (figure 8-3). As Peters (1993) notes, worldwide trends suggest less liquid cargo, steeper proportional increases in dry cargo volumes, and a steady growth in general cargo in international sea trade. These trends in dry bulk goods and general cargo are reflected in Rotterdam, but the declines in liquid cargo have not occurred. The large volume of petroleum passing through Rotterdam (with appropriate complementary investments on land and physical facilities by the port) has enabled it to become a major petrochemical industrial complex. The general cargo, particularly container traffic, while growing, is less significant in Rotterdam than in leading Asian ports. Rotterdam is the fourth largest container port in the world behind Singapore, Hong Kong and Kaoshsiung (figure 8-4).

Of the 10,000 hectares that form the total port area, half is land, which is split between industry and a massive infrastructure of railroads, highways, pipelines, and storage tanks. Industrial development has been an important part of port activities at Rotterdam. Much of the oil landed in the port is processed at one of the four refineries at the port, while 50

Figure 8-2. World's Major Cargo Ports, 1995–98

Millions of metric tons

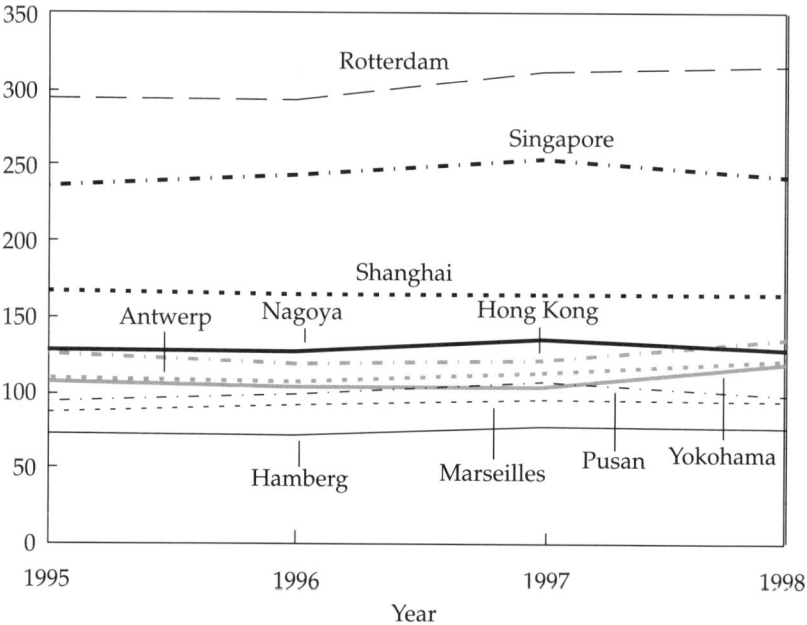

Source: Rotterdam Port Information Centre, February 2000.

percent is piped to Flushing, Antwerp, or Germany (Port of Rotterdam, 1998). The refinery and chemical industries that dominate the port in-dustrial complex are being buffeted by technical and organizational change, at a time when the broader economic context for port and mari-time activities is also in flux.

Rotterdam: Strategic Positioning in the Global Transport Networks

The Changing Center and Scope of the Global Transport Networks

Changes in the global transport networks and in the Rotterdam port in particular derive from two broad sources: transformations in the *produc-tion system* and transformations in the *transportation system*. The former has three important elements: globalization of manufacturing services;

Figure 8-3. Total Throughput by Commodity at Port Rotterdam, 1995–98

Millions of metric tons

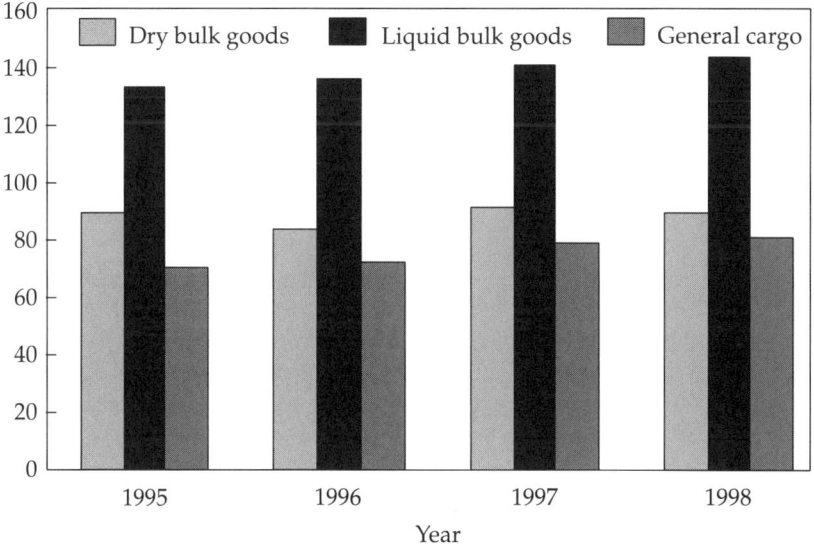

Source: Rotterdam Port Information Centre, February 2000.

volatility of demand because of production system changes; and the shift to high-value production and outsourcing.

Globalization of manufacturing services is driven by the search among OECD countries for countries offering lower factor costs. As a result, in the past two decades many intermediate manufacturing and assembly activities have relocated to developing countries. Likely consequences of this trend (in the context of a trend toward inventory reduction) are twofold: diminishing demand for long-haul ocean transport of many primary commodities from developing countries to industrialized economies and greater demand for small, high-value, speedy shipments.

The "half-life" of an increasing number of products is shortening, and new products appear quickly, with important consequences for transportation. The inputs and outputs of production will rapidly change as well as the locations where they must be transported to and from. The challenge for Rotterdam, if it is to maintain its leadership, is to prepare

Figure 8-4. World's Major Container Ports, 1995–98

Thousands of TEUs

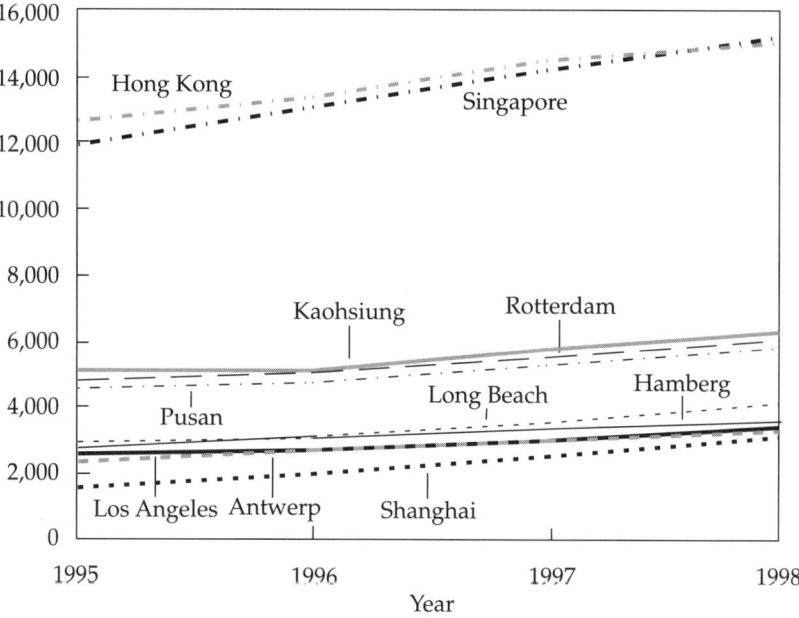

Year

Source: Rotterdam Port Information Centre, February 2000.

for such rapid changes in the volume, composition, and flow patterns of global cargo.

With increasing globalization and competitive pressures, there is a growing trend among firms to focus on core businesses and outsource many activities. This has two consequences: first, in the chemical industry, chemical firms are locating in close proximity to one another because of cost and efficiency of operations; second, the production shifts in this industry (in a high-income economy such as the Netherlands) toward the components and products that add higher value. In the increasingly roundabout production process, intensified cooperation between suppliers and purchasers is becoming even more essential. In this context, the Rotterdam port, which is a major chemical complex, must offer opportunities for such clustering and cooperation among the tenant firms in order to gain dynamic competitive advantages.

With regard to major changes in the transportation system, reorganization of the distribution function is particularly noteworthy. As globalization increases, transport operations expand in scale, and supply management systems elaborate and differentiate. Ports that act strategically have new opportunities to be locations of higher-order strategic business chains that concentrate distribution activities for Europe-wide operations.

In addition, institutional arrangements in port operations are changing. As port ownership and operations are liberalized, ports companies own and operate ports and related functions in other parts of the world, and innovative cooperative enterprises develop among ports, shipping companies, logistical firms, and industrial port tenants. This, in turn, affects the scope of operations of ports like Rotterdam.

Adaptive Restructuring in Rotterdam

It is against the backdrop of such changes in the global production and transport networks that Rotterdam (and other pro-active ports such as Singapore and Hong Kong) improve services to their customers and industrial tenants and form strategic alliances with large transport companies and multinational corporations. The goal is to promote future distribution functions and to reinforce existing markets as well as create new ones in its hinterland.

Rotterdam offers safe movement annually to more than 29,000 vessels, including some of the largest vessels (draft of 57 feet or more). It uses a variety of sophisticated information systems, including INDRIS (Inland Navigation Demonstrator for River Information Services). These systems can be utilized by terminals, inland shipping operators, and customs and other transport-chain service providers. The port engages in knowledge-intensive operations, and it participates in creating new port knowledge infrastructure. Examples of such participation are the design of a container terminal of the future, a value-added dry bulk logistics project, and SIMLOG, a project focused on simulation techniques for logistics processes (RMPM, 1998).

In addition, the port of Rotterdam and the corporate sector participate jointly in the Information Technology (IT) project of Port Community Rotterdam (PCR). PCR is focused on the creation of a faster, smarter design for a container transport logistical chain by developing, simulating, implementing, and managing port-wide information technology applications (RMPM, 1998). Such applications include Cargo Card, EDI-LAND, and ITmagination. The Cargo Card is an electronic card that rapidly identifies people and containers and cuts down on fraud. EDI-LAND is aimed at a uniform code for electronic messages among the corporate and public sectors. ITmagination is aimed at generating information and demonstrations of the proper use of information technology in transport and logistics for small and medium-size enterprises. Such investments in knowledge and competencies on the part of Rotterdam port reflect its shift from a transport facility that mainly ships, stores, and processes raw materials to a center that engages in "added value" distribution and logistical management activities and coordinates the movement of cargo around the world.

This ongoing transformation of Rotterdam into a knowledge-intensive hub of a global transport system is greatly promoted by concurrent institutional changes in the world's maritime industry. With the privatization of ports and related activities, pro-active ports and stevedoring firms are responding to the increased scale of operations in the wake of globalization by ownership of other ports, firm mergers, and a variety of alliances. The Port of Singapore Authority took equity positions in the ports of Venice and Genoa in 1998 (RMPM, 1998). Hutchinson International Port Holdings of Hong Kong took over the port of Thamesport in England, and the Associated British Port Authority bought American Port Services. Hutchinson is to obtain a 50 percent stake in Rotterdam's container terminal, which in turn has acquired the operating rights to a container terminal in Trieste, Italy, and has developed new inland terminals in Belgium, Germany, and the Netherlands (RMPM, 1998).

The resulting competition and complex collaboration among ports, stevedoring firms, and shipping firms are not only lowering transport operating costs but also creating new port products and functions that are adaptive responses to the emerging transport world. Three adaptive responses in Rotterdam will be described here. The first is the positioning of Rotterdam as the strategic location for business chains that are Europe-wide and worldwide. Rotterdam set up the new Distripark Maasvlakte (the largest of the three Distriparks in the port) as the locale for such activities. This Distripark is located directly across from the large container terminals on the Maasvlakte, and it is linked by an internal track (RMPM, 1998). The port is recruiting firms that want to set up their European distribution activities, large carriers that want to penetrate farther into the logistical chain, mega-distributors on the lookout for a hub for their European operations, and European exporters and other logistical service providers. The early tenants include Reebok, which opened its European Distribution Center (EDC); Eurofrigo, a subsidiary of (the Japanese) Nicherei Foods; and (the American) ProLogis, the world's largest owner and operator of distribution space. These arrivals will strengthen capabilities in existing facilities. For example, Schenker, one of the world's leading shipping agents and logistical provider, is building its European hub in Rotterdam. To speed up the larger cargo volumes that are expected, the customs function at the port is being reformed. Dutch Customs, which has its largest office in the country at the Distripark Maasvlakte, is equipped with a container-scanning device so that entire trucks, including their container, can be checked in a few minutes.

The second example of adaptive restructuring in Rotterdam is the changing composition of the port's industrial activities: Rotterdam is moving toward higher value-adding activities. Approximately 60 percent of the port and its industrial complex is used for the handling of crude oil and petroleum products and chemical industry. As noted earlier, the trends in the chemical industry toward high value adding and outsourcing encourage the firms to locate their operations near one another. By promoting cooperation, co-siting, and clustering among the firms at the port, Rotterdam is attempting to transform itself from a refinery port to a chemical port that can attract firms such as Eastman.

Third, Rotterdam is not only strengthening existing hinterland connections but also making strategic investments that create new markets. An example of the former objective is to maintain and improve port accessibility to the hinterland by encouraging a shift in the modal split from roads to railroads and inland shipping. Table 8-2 indicates this shift in the container modal split between 1994 and 1998. The share of road transport declined during this period from 64 percent to 52 percent. The increased use of rail and inland waterway transport will improve accessibility from the port and the industrial area, and it will benefit both the natural environment and working and living environments.

Rotterdam's investment in CSKD-Intrans, the Czech Republic's railroad operator, exemplifies its strategic actions to create new markets. A Rotterdam consortium comprising the Municipal Port, the container company, and Eurotrafo holds 79 percent of the shares of the Czech railroad that operates many rail terminals in the Czech and Slovak Republics—in this manner strengthening its hinterland position. Ports such as Bremen and Hamburg have taken similar actions.

Table 8-2. Container Modal Split at Rotterdam

(percent)

Year	Rail	Inland shipping	Road
1994	9	27	64
1995	10	30	60
1996	11	31	58
1997	13	34	53
1998	13	35	52

Source: RMPM (1998, 9).

Conclusions

Rotterdam is a major transportation facility that has remained at the forefront of transportation activities for nearly four decades. Rotterdam's dynamism and preeminence over this long period are a tribute to its performance and strategic alertness. The port has clearly understood the influential forces in the larger environment and the factors that underlie the success of a major transport hub. The port has identified a workable adaptive strategy and reinvented itself in each new era with appropriate physical, human, and institutional investments.

Rotterdam's approach has been twofold: first, the organization of the relevant knowledge and competencies in order to provide the state-of-the-art trade-transport chain services to its customers; second, continuous reinvention of its role and functions in the context of emerging change. Lessons from the Rotterdam experience should be instructive for the managers of ports and airports in many developing countries. Such managers could build on Rotterdam's knowledge and competencies as they organize trade-transport chain services in their facilities.

References

Aghion, Philippe, Eve Caroli, and Cecilia Garcia-Penalosa. 1999. "Inequality and Economic Growth: The Perspective of the New Growth Theories." *Journal of Economic Literature* 37 (December): 1615–60.

Amjadi, A., and L. Alan Winters. 1997. "Transport Costs and "Natural Integration in Mercosur." Policy Research Working Paper 1742. World Bank, Washington, D.C.

Anas, A., and K. S. Lee. 1988. "Infrastructure Investment and Productivity: The Case of Nigerian Manufacturing." World Bank Discussion Paper. Washington, D.C.

Anas, A., K. S. Lee, and M. Murray. 1996. "Industrial Bottlenecks, Private Provision, and Industrial Productivity." Policy Research Working Paper 1603. World Bank, Operations Evaluation Department, Infrastructure and Energy Division, Washington, D.C.

Bandara, J. S., and M. McGillivray. 1998. "Trade Policy Reforms in South Asia." London: Blackwell.

Bereskin, C. Gregory. 1996. "Econometric Estimation of the Effects of Deregulation on Railway Productivity Growth." *Transportation Journal* 35 (4): 34–43.

Borenstein, Severin. 1992. "The Evolution of Airline Competition." *Journal of Economic Perspectives* 6 (2): 45–73.

Bougheas, Spiros, P.O. Demetrades, and E.L.W. Morgenroth. 1999. "Infrastructure, Costs and Trade." *Journal of Development Economics* 47: 169–89.

Boyer, Kenneth D. 1997. *Principles of Transportation Economics*. New York: Addison-Wesley.

Brown, W. Mark, and William P. Anderson. 1999a. "The Influence of Industrial and Spatial Structure on Canada-U.S. Regional Trade." *Growth and Change* 30 (1): 23–47.

———. 1999b. "The Potential for Economic Integration among Canadian and American Regions." McMaster University, Department of Geography, Hamilton, Ontario, Canada.

Button, Kenneth. 1993. "The Future of European Transport." In Roland Thord, ed., *The Future of Transportation and Communication: Visions and Perspectives from Europe, Japan, and the USA.* Berlin: Springer-Verlag.

Chow, Garland. 1997. "North American Trucking Policy." In T. H. Oum and others, eds., *Transport Economics,* 591–624. Amsterdam: Harwood Academic Publishers.

Chow, Garland, and J. J. McRae. 1989. "Nontariff Barriers and the Structure of the U.S.-Canadian (Transborder) Trucking Industry." *Transportation Journal* 30 (2): 4–21.

Coffey, Peter. 1998. *Mercosur.* Norwell, Mass.: Kluwer Academic Publishers.

De Araujo, J. T., and Luis Tineo. 1998. "Harmonising of Competetion Policies among Mercosur Countries." *Antitrust Bulletin* 43 (1): 45–70.

Delaney, Robert V. 1993. "Transportation, Regulation and International Trade." In G. P. O'Driscoll Jr., ed., *Free Trade within North America,* 161. Norwell, Mass.: Kluewer Publishing Co.

Development Bank of Southern Africa. 1998. *Maputo Development Corridor, www.dbsa.org/Development Corridors/Corridors/maputo/sectiona.htm.*

Dick, Malise. 1992. *Trade Facilitation and Transport Reform.* Report 25. World Bank, Latin American and the Carribbean Technical Department, Washington, D.C.

Douglas, George W., and James C. Miller III. 1974. "Quality Competition, Industry Equilibrium and Efficiency in the Price-Constrained Airline Market." *The American Economic Review* 657–69.

Dyer, Philip. 1996. "Ports of Call." *Town and Country Planning,* 255–56.

European Commission. 1993. *White Paper on Growth, Competitiveness, and Employment: The Challenges and Ways Forward into the Twenty-first Century.*

————. 1998. Directorate General for Transport. *Transeuropean Networks: State of Play of the Fourteen Priority Projects.* www.curopa.cu.int/comm/transport/themes/network/english/tentpp9807/tentpp9807.html.

————. 1999. Directorate General for Transport. Guide to the Transport Acquis. October. www.europa.eu.int/en/comm/dg07/enlargement/index.htm.

————. 2000a. Directorate General for Energy and Transport. *EU Transport in Figures: Statistical Pocketbook.* January.

————. 2000b. *Report from the Commission on the Implementation of Regulation (EEC) No. 3118/93.* www.europa.eu.int/eur-lex/en/com/pdf/2000/com2000_0105en01.pdf.

————. no date. *The Common Transport Policy Sustainable Mobility: Perspectives for the Future.* Commission communication to the Council, European Parliament, Economic and Social Committee and Committee of the Regions.

Federal Highway Administration. 1998. *North American Initiatives.* Washington, D.C.: U.S. Department of Transportation. Spring.

Francois, J. F., and others. 1996. "Commercial Policy and the Domestic Carrying Trade." *Canadian Journal of Economics* 29 (1): 181–98.

Frankel, Jeffrey A. 1997. *Regional Trading Blocs.* Washington, D.C.: Institute for International Economics.

Gartner, Lou Branco. 1999. "Rotterdam Port." Paper presented at the World Bank/ESCAP Regional Technical Workshop on Transport and Transit Facilitation, Bangkok. April, 1999.

Gomez-Ibanez, Jose A. 1997. *Privatizing Transport in Argentina.* Kennedy School of Government Case Program, Harvard University, Cambridge, Mass.

Harris, N. 1994. "The Emerging Global City." *Cites,* 332–36.

Helliwell, J. F. 1996. "Do National Borders Matter for Quebec Trade?" *Canadian Journal of Economics* 24: 507–22.

Hirst, Monica. 1999. "Merosur's Complex Political Agenda." In Riorden Roett, ed., *Mercosur: Regional Integration, World Markets,* 35–47. Boulder, Colo.: Lynne Rienner Publishers.

Hossain, M., I. Islam, R. Kibria. 1998. *The South Asian Economies: Transformation, Opportunities, and Challenges.* London: Routledge.

IMF (International Monetary Fund). 1999a. *Direction of Trade Statistics.* Washington, D.C.

————. 1999b. *International Financial Statistics Yearbook.* Washington, D.C.

Kaombwe, Smak. 1998. "Transport Integration and Facilitation in Southern Africa: SADC Strategy, Experience, and Future Perspectives." Paper presented at the World Bank/ESCAP Regional Technical Workshop on Transport and Transit Facilitation, Bangkok. April, 1999.

Kinnock, Neil. 1995. "The Private Sector's Role in Development of TENS." Speech by the Directorate General for Transport to the European Investment Bank Conference, Amsterdam. May 18.

Kopicki, Ronald J. (ed.). 2000. *Best Policies and Practices for Supply Chain Development in Emerging Markets.* Boston, Mass.: MIT Press.

Krugman, Paul R. 1979. "Increasing Returns, Monopolistic Competition, and International Trade." *American Economic Review* 70: 950–59.

————. 1998. "The Role of Geography in Development." Paper presented at the annual World Bank Conference on Development Economics.

Kuznets, Simon. 1955. "Economic Growth and Income Inequality." *American Economic Review* 45: 1–28.

Lakshmanan, T. R., and William P. Anderson. 1999. "Trade and Transport Integration: Lessons from the North American Experience." Paper presented at the World Bank/ESCAP Regional Technical Workshop on Transport and Transit Facilitation, Bangkok. April, 1999.

Leautier, Frannie A. 1999. "Transport in South Asia: Issues and Options." Paper presented at the World Bank/ESCAP Regional Technical Workshop on Transport and Transit Facilitation, Bangkok. April, 1999.

Linfield, Michael. 1999. "Maputo Corridor Study: Australia Housing and Urban Research Institute." Queensland University of Technology.

Manzetti, Luigi. 1994. "The Political Economy of Mercosur." *Journal of Interamerican Studies and World Affairs,* 101–41.

Markwald, Ricardo, and J. B. Machado. 1999. "Establishing an Industrial Policy for Mercosur." In *Mercosur: Regional Integration, World Markets,* 63–80. Boulder, Colo.: Lynne Rienner Publishers.

Maxwell, T. 1999. "Impediments to Exporting." Paper presented at the World Bank/ESCAP Regional Technical Workshop on Transport and Transit Facilitation, Bangkok. April, 1999.

McCallum, J. 1995. "National Borders Matter: U.S.-Canada Regional Trade Patterns." *American Economic Review* 85: 615–23.

McCormick, John. 1999. *Understanding the European Union.* New York: St. Martin's Press.

Meyer, John R., and others. 1959. *The Economics of Competition in the Transportation Industries.* Cambridge, Mass.: Harvard University Press.

Montufar, Jeannette. 1996. *Trucking and Size and Weight Regulations in the Mid-Continent Corridor.* Master of Science Thesis, Department of Civil and Geological Engineering, University of Manitoba, Winnipeg.

Morrison, Steven A., and Clifford Winston. 1999. "Regulatory Reform of U.S. Intercity Transportation." In Jose A. Gomez-Ibanez, B. Tye, and Clifford Winston, eds., *Essays in Transportation Economics and Policy.* Washington, D.C.: Brookings Institution Press.

Motor Vehicle Projects Office, John A. Volpe National Transportation Systems Center. 1996. *ITS/CVO Cross-Border Strategic Plan.* Report prepared for Federal Highway Administration, U.S. Department of Transportation. July.

Mye, Randy, and L. Palagonia. 1996. "Mercosur's Potential Market." *Business America August* vol. 117, no. 8.

Nadiri, M. Ishaq, and Theofanis P. Mamuneas. 1994. "R & D Investments and the Growth of Factor Productivity in U.S. Manufacturing Industries." Working Paper W4845. Cambridge, Mass.: National Bureau of Economic Research. August.

National Transportation Act Review Commission (Canada). 1993. *Competition in Transportation Policy Legislation in Review,* vols. 1, 2. Ottawa Minister of Supply in Services, Canada.

North American Free Trade Agreement Land Transportation Standards Subcommittee. 1997. *Harmonization of Vehicle Weight* and *Dimensions Regulations within the NAFTA Partnership.* Report of Working Group 2, Vehicle Weights and Dimensions. October.

NRC (National Research Council) Transportation Research Board. 1991. *Winds of Change: Domestic Air Transport since Deregulation,* Special Report 230. Washington, D.C.

OECD (Organization for Economic Cooperation and Development). 1998. *Implications of the Mercosur Agreement for Cereal and Livestock Product Markets and Trade.* Directorate for Food and Agriculture AGR/CA (98) 4 Final.

Ohlin, B. 1933. *Interregional and International Trade.* Cambridge, Mass. Harvard University Press.

O'Reilly, Dolores, and Alec Stone Sweet. 1998. "The Liberalization and European Reregulation of Air Transport." In Wayne Sandholtz and Alec Stone Sweet, eds., *European Integration and Supranational Governance.* Oxford: Oxford University Press.

Parkash, M. R. 2000."Container Trade in Bangladesh: An Overview." Working Paper 8. Prepared for the World Bank Study *Forging Subregional Links in Transportation and Logistics in South Asia.* See Subramanian and Arnold (2001).

Pereira, Lia V. 1999. "Towards the Common Market of the South: Mercosur's Origins, Evolution, and Challenges." In *Mercosur: Regional Integration, World Markets,* 7–23. Boulder, Colo.: Lynne Rienner Publishers.

Peters, Hans J. 1993. *The Maritime Transport Crisis.* World Bank Discussion Paper 220. Washington, D.C.

Pigato, M., and others. 1997. *South Asia's Integration into the World Economy.* Washington, D.C.: World Bank.

Port of Rotterdam. 1998a. "Rotterdam—A Dynamic Port for Industry." *Chemical Week Custom Publication,* June 17, 4–16

———. 1998b. *Rotterdam: Mainport Europe.*

Prentice, Barry E., and William W. Wilson. 1998. "Future Transportation Developments in the U.S./Canada/Mexico Grain-Livestock Subsector under NAFTA and WTO." In R. M. A. Loyns, Ronald D. Knutson, and Karl Meilke, eds., *Economic Harmonization in the Canadian/U.S./Mexico Grain-Livestock Subsector,* Proceedings of the Fourth Agricultural and Food Policy Systems Information Workshop, December. Winnipeg, MB: Friesen Printers.

Prud'homme, Remy. 1995. "The Dangers of Decentralisation." *World Bank Research Observer* 10:2 (August).

Rahman, Mustafizur. 1996. "Regional Trade Cooperation in the SAARC: Issues of Transition from SAPTA to SAFTA." Paper presented at the regional seminar on the South Asia Free Trade Area organized by the SAARC Chamber of Commerce in Dhaka, December 17.

RMPM (Rotterdam Municipal Port Management). 1998. *Annual Report.*

Roett, Riorden. 1999. "Introduction." In Riorden Roett, ed., *Mercosur: Regional Integration, World Markets,* 1–6. Boulder, Colo.: Lynne Rienner Publishers.

Safadi, Raed, and Alexander Yeats. 1993. "The North American Free Trade Agreement: Its Effect on South Asia." Policy Research Working Paper 1119. World Bank, Washington, D.C.

Schware, Robert, and Paul Kimberly. 1995. "Information Technology and National Trade Facilitation." Technical Paper 316. World Bank, Washington, D.C.

Snow, John W. 1977. "The Problem of Motor Carrier Regulation and the Ford Administration's Proposal for Reform." In Paul W. MacAvoy and John W. Snow, eds., *Regulation of Entry and Pricing in Truck Transportation,* 3–46. Washington, D.C.: American Enterprise Institute.

Sowinski, Lara L. 2000. "Is There a Perfect Logistics Product in the Market?" *World Trade* (February): 32–36.

Strah, T. M. 1995. "Mexican Truckers Set off Alarms." *Transport Topics,* March 13, 7.

Subramanian, Uma, 1999. "South Asia Transport: Issues and Options." Paper presented at the World Bank/ESCAP Regional Technical Workshop on Transport and Transit Facilitation, Bangkok. April, 1999.

Subramanian, Uma, and John Arnold. 2001. *Forging Subregional Links in Transport and Logistics in South Asia.* Washington, D.C.: World Bank.

Trans African Concessions. no date. N4 Project Outline, www.tracn4.co.za

Transport Canada. 1998. *Transportation in Canada 1997: Annual Report.* Minister of Public Works and Government Services, Canada.

UNCHS (United Nations Centre for Human Settlements). 1995a. Global Urban Observatory Database.

———. 1995b. Urban Indicators Program.

U.S. Department of Commerce. various years. *U.S. Foreign Trade Highlights.* Washington, D.C. U.S. Government Printing Office.

U.S. Department of Transportation. 1997a. *Comprehensive Truck Size and Weight Study,* vol. 2: *Issues and Background.* Washington, D.C.: U.S. Government Printing Office.

————. 1997b. Bureau of Transportation Statistics. *Transportation Statistics Annual Report.*

U.S. General Accounting Office. 1990. *Report on Fares and Reduced Competition at Concentrated Airports.* GAO/ RCED-90102. Washington, D.C.: U.S. Government Printing Office.

————. 1996. *Commercial Trucking: Safety and Infrastructure Issues under the North American Free Trade Agreement.* GAO/RCED-96–61. February.

————. 1997a. *Commercial Passenger Vehicles: Safety Inspection of Commercial Buses and Vans Entering the United States from Mexico.* GAO/RCED–97–194. August.

————. 1997b. *Commercial Trucking: Safety Concerns about Mexican Trucks Remain Even as Inspection Activity Increases.* GAO/RCED–97–68. April.

Verghese, B. G. 1996. *India Northeast Resurgent: Ethnicity, Insurgency, Governance, Development.* Report for the Center for Policy Research. New Delhi: Konark Publishers.

von Klaudy, Stephan. 1999a. "Southern Africa Transport Corridor." Paper presented at the World Bank/ESCAP Regional Technical Workshop on Transport and Transit Facilitation, Bangkok. April, 1999.

————. 1999b. "Topical Note: Maputo Corridor." Internal World Bank document. Washington, D.C.

Winston, Clifford, 1985. "Conceptual Developments in the Economics of Transportation: An Interpretive Survey." *Journal of Economic Literature* 23: 83

Winston, Clifford, Thomas Corsi, and Curtis Grimm. 1990. *The Economic Effects of Surface Freight Deregulation.* Washington, D.C.: The Brookings Institution Press.

World Bank. 1994. *World Development Report.* New York: Oxford University Press.

————. 1995. "Improving African Transport Corridors." Operations Evaluation Department, Precis Number 84. Washington, D.C.

————. 1999a. "Proceedings of the Regional Private Sector Consultative Meeting: Regional Initiative on Transport Integration." Background Note. See Subramanian and Arnold. *Forging Subregional Links in Transportation and Logistics in South Asia.*

————. 1999b. Proceedings of Regional Technical Workshop on Transport and Transit Facilitation. World Bank-UN ESCAP Workshop in Bangkok, 1999. Washington, D.C.

————. 1999c. *World Development Indicators.* Washington, D.C.

————. 2000a. *Cities in Transition: Urban and Local Government Strategy.* Infrastructure Group, Urban Development. Washington, D.C.

————. 2000b. *Entering the Twenty-first Century: World Development Report 1999–2000.* New York: Oxford University Press.

————. 2000c. *World Development Indicators.* Washington, D.C.

Yeats, Alexander. 1997. "Does Mercosur's Trade Performance Raise Concerns about the Effects of Regional Trade Arrangements?" Policy Research Working Paper 1729. World Bank, Washington, D.C.

Yergin, Daniel, and Joseph Stanislaw. 1998. *The Commanding Heights: The Battle between Government and the Marketplace that is Remaking the Modern World.* New York: Simon and Schuster.

Zinn, Walter. 1999. *Supply Chain Efficiency in a Trade Bloc Environment: Three Cases in Mercosur.* Draft report.